20 YEARS

20 Years Too Soon
Prelude to Major-League Integrated Baseball

Quincy Trouppe

Missouri Historical Society Press • Saint Louis

Acknowledgments

I hope baseball fans all over the world who read my book will thoroughly understand why I had to write it. I identify myself and many other blacks with a poem written by Dave Malarcher. In the poem, a beautiful flower grows in the middle of the jungle, never seen by the outside world. After playing one year with the Cleveland Indians, during my twenty-second year of playing and managing professional baseball, I know I could have had several great years in the big leagues had I been able to start earlier.

I'd like to express my gratitude to the following men who made great records for themselves in baseball and found the time to write giving their opinions of my ability:

Birdie Tebbetts, Major League Manager
Monte Irvin, Baseball Commissioner's Office
Joe Black, Major League Pitcher
Bob Feller, Major League Pitcher
Bernardo Pasquel, Mexico City Club (Owner)

In addition, I would like to say something about the editor of my book. Tariq Muhammad has done a great job in helping me prepare it. I'm very grateful to him.

I also wish to thank Dr. Sam Shepard for his Foreword. Growing up in St. Louis, he saw me play and is familiar with my athletic career. Dr. Shepard was an outstanding athlete himself and officiated for many years as a referee around the country.

PREFACE

From the time I was ten years old and a student at L'Overture Elementary School in St. Louis, Missouri, the most important part of my life has been centered around baseball. For me, baseball was something like a mother, father, and best friend, all rolled into one. When I felt low and disgusted with everything, it gave me a lift. When I was riding high and the wind of glory was caressing my ears, it brought me down to earth.

I started going to see the St. Louis Stars play when I was twelve. They were a member of the Negro National League. Because I did not have even a dime to spend, I had to figure out a way into the park. It didn't take long; I soon learned to hustle balls, the rule being that anyone returning a ball fouled over the stands into the street would be admitted free. I had a special spot that really seemed to hold luck for me, and I always got my ball, though sometimes the game was well under way before I got in.

Looking back, I realize I watched everything that went on during those hard-to-come-by games and through them learned baseball at an early age. I know what I observed there was a great help to me in starting pro ball as a young man.

The men I watched were real professionals and knew how to play, but most were not quick to give a youngster a helping hand. A young player had it rough. The kids then had to have guts, or they failed to become players. The experienced players would not tell a youngster how to make a play, but when a mistake was made by the rookie, there was hell. It was even harder being a young black player, because most blacks did not have much of a future in the game. I suppose the only reason I even entered baseball professionally was because of my love for the game.

My greatest years in baseball were from 1932 to 1943. During that time I played with some of the finest black teams in North and Latin America; some of the most colorful years of my baseball life were with teams in Mexico, Puerto Rico, and Venezuela, as well as the United States. Because the Negro League did not keep a day-to-day record of its players, I have made use of newspaper clippings of that period to recall my activities. However, the records were well maintained in Mexico and Puerto Rico, and they show that I gained several high honors during the years I played in Latin America.

In 1933, when the Bismarck, North Dakota, season ended early, I finally had a chance to see a game between white players, a game played at Sportsman Park in St. Louis. I was never so let down. Though I never saw Babe Ruth, Lou Gehrig, Ty Cobb, George Sisler, Harry Hielman, Al Simmons, Jimmy Foxx, Lefty Grove, or many of the others play, I had grown up accepting the idea that white baseball was superior to black. I was expecting to see a ball club of white players perform in a way much superior to the caliber of baseball I had been playing.

I had even heard many Negro fans say that Negroes could not play well enough to get into the big leagues, but my experience in the Negro League gave me a chance to come in contact with all kinds of people, including whites who said that the Negroes who ran down black players were wrong. I heard many whites say if certain black players had been white they would be stars in the majors.

After watching the game that day in Bismarck, I was absolutely sure that I played well enough to be in the majors. I played as well as any of the players I had seen that afternoon, but they were white and I was black. I knew I had a great arm. I could think, I had good hands, and I could run faster than the average player. I know, had I been given the opportunity, I would have had a great record in major-league baseball.

In 1944 my big wish to manage a pro baseball club came true. I managed for seven years in the United States and Latin America. In 1952 I gave up being a player-manager after receiving an offer to play with the Cleveland Indians. It was at this time, over twenty years after my start in professional baseball, that I got into a major-league park for the first time. For all of my life, the radio had been as close as I had ever been to a big-league park; the great white baseball players of my childhood days moved in a world I did not know. The impossible dream of playing in the majors was fulfilled then in 1952, though too late, and for too short a time.

In 1953 I signed to scout for the St. Louis Cardinals. I scouted twelve years for the team, and during that time I recommended the signing of such players as Ernie Banks, Roberto Clemente, Vic Power, and Frank Herrera, all of whom have made good in the big leagues.

In spite of the frustrations of the color barrier, baseball opened doors for me that would have been barred otherwise. It brought me into contact with some of the greatest players in the game. It revealed new vistas that were more educational than a doctor's degree.

Because of this great national game, I have lived a life comparable to the wealthiest people in the United States. There were tears, too. But the happiness and the sadness always blended into something that made my life more complete.

In this book, I have brought all of these experiences—happy and sad—together so that today's fans will be able to appreciate what had to be overcome to enjoy a world of integrated baseball. I hope that you will enjoy reading about my years in baseball as much I have enjoyed playing the game.

Quincy Trouppe
1977

POEM FOR MY FATHER

BY QUINCY TROUPE, JR.

father, it was an honor to be there, in the dugout
with you, the glory of great black men swinging their lives
as bats, at tiny white balls
burning in at unbelievable speeds, riding up & in & out
a curve breaking down wicked, like a ball falling off a table
moving away, snaking down, screwing its stitched magic
into chitling circuit air, its comma seams spinning
toward breakdown, dipping, like a hipster
bebopping a knee-dip stride, in the charlie parker forties
wrist curling, like a swan's neck
behind a slick black back
cupping an invisible ball of dreams

& you there, father, regal, as an african, obeah man
sculpted out of wood, from a sacred tree, of no name, no place, origin
thick branches branching down, into cherokee & someplace else lost
way back in africa, the sap running dry
crossing from north carolina into georgia, inside grandmother mary's
womb, where your mother had you in the violence of that red soil
ink blotter news, gone now, into blood graves
of american blues, sponging rococo
truth long gone as dinosaurs
the agent-oranged landscape of former names
absent of african polysyllables, dry husk consonants there
now, in their place, names, flat, as polluted rivers
& that guitar string smile always snaking across
some virulent, american, redneck's face
scorching, like atomic heat, mushrooming over nagasaki
& hiroshima, the fever blistered shadows of it all
inked, as etchings, into sizzled concrete

but you, there, father, through it all, a yardbird solo
riffing on bat & ball glory, breaking down the fabricated myths
of white major league legends, of who was better than who
beating them at their own crap game, with killer bats,
as bud powell swung his silence into beauty of a josh
gibson home run, skittering across piano keys of bleachers
shattering all manufactured legends up there in lights
struck out white knights, on the risky edge of amazement

XV

awe, the miraculous truth sluicing through
steeped & disguised in the blues
confluencing, like the point at the cross
when a fastball hides itself up in a slider, curve
breaking down & away in a wicked, sly grin
curved & posed as an ass-scratching uncle tom, who
like old sachel paige delivering his famed hesitation pitch
before coming back with a hard, high, fast one, is slicker
sliding, & quicker than a professional hitman—
the deadliness of it all, the sudden strike
like that of the "brown bomber's" crossing right
of sugar ray robinson's, lightning, cobra bite

& you, there, father, through it all, catching rhythms of chono
pozo balls, drumming, like conga beats into your catcher's mitt
hard & fast as "cool papa" bell jumping into bed
before the lights went out

of the old, negro baseball league, a promise, you were
father, a harbinger, of shock waves, soon come

20 Years Too Soon

INTRODUCTION
THE GENTLEMAN QUINCY TROUPPE, AS I KNEW HIM
BY LARRY LESTER

Quincy Thomas "Big Train" Trouppe was not a superstar baseball player. He was an exceptional athlete, who, when given the opportunity, excelled at America's national pastime.

Quincy was born on Christmas day, 1912. William Howard Taft was in the White House, the Boston Red Sox had beaten the New York Giants in the World Series, and the statue of Queen Nefertiti had just been discovered in Egypt. At the time, milk for baby Quincy was thirty-four cents a gallon, and a loaf of bread cost a liberty-head nickel.

At a young age, his family moved to St. Louis, Missouri, were he attended Toussaint L'Overture Elementary School and later graduated from Vashon High School. He attended Lincoln University in Jefferson City, Missouri, for two years.

Quincy's years in professional baseball began in 1930, when he joined the St. Louis Stars as a pitcher, fresh out of high school. In his debut game against the Detroit Stars, he threw four innings and only gave up one hit. For his initial efforts he was paid eighty dollars a month, plus two dollars a day for meals. The Stars soon discovered he was a better hitter than pitcher, though, and converted him to catcher, officially signing him to the team in 1931. He played one more year with the Stars before the effects of the Great Depression broke up the Negro Leagues.

The 1932 season found Trouppe making whistle stops with the Detroit Wolves, Kansas City Monarchs, and the Homestead Grays. Ninety-three-year-old Ted "Double Duty" Radcliffe remembers the rookie Trouppe as "always a gentleman. He was one of the better young catchers to come along. He could catch and throw that ball. He was also one of the better hitters, a dangerous hitter. You couldn't fool him at the plate. Yeah, he was a good ball player. He was a number-one ball player in my book."

As black baseball was recovering from the depression woes, Quincy found other paths to display his athletic abilities, traveling the AAU boxing circuit. Just before opening day of the 1936 season, Trouppe won the AAU Junior

Heavyweight Championship in Providence, Rhode Island, defeating Jimmy Robinson from Philadelphia for the crown. He was awarded the Governor Theodore Francis Green Trophy for his efforts. 1936 was also his last year playing baseball with the semipro Bismarck, North Dakota, Cubs, where he had played since 1933. Disgruntled with segregated life in professional baseball, he regretfully retired in 1937. The next year, he received a call from the Indianapolis ABCs, with whom he spent two seasons, but the brief tour was only a recurrence of the tough travel schedule of black baseball in America.

In 1939 Quincy married his high-school sweetheart, Dorothy Smith, but soon after left the States for a baseball career in Mexico. From 1939 to 1944, Trouppe found solace and fame there, batting over .300 each season he played, first with the Monterrey Carta Blanca team (1939-41) and then the Mexican City Reds (1942-44). It was while playing in Mexico that Quincy learned of the birth of his two sons back at home—Quincy, Jr., in '39, and Timothy in '41. A daughter, Stephanie, would be born to a second marriage in 1953.

Life and baseball were fairly free from racial prejudice in Mexico, allowing Quincy to refine his managerial skills. It was also in Mexico that he decided to change his last name from *Troupe* to *Trouppe*. Though Quincy, Jr., has speculated that this may have been a small attempt to create a new identity in Mexico, Quincy, Sr.'s, own reasoning was straightforward: "My family always spelled it with one *p*, but when I went to Mexico, they spelled it with two *p*s and pronounced my name 'Troo-pay.' I liked the way it sounded and I've used it ever since." In this revised edition of *20 Years Too Soon*, the name *Troupe* is used until 1946, about the time he changed the name; in this Introduction, I have used *Trouppe*, because that is how I knew the man.

In 1944, Trouppe hesitantly joined the Cleveland Buckeyes, owned by Erie, Pennsylvania, hotel owner Ernest Wright. The next year as manager, Quincy reached the pinnacle of his career. Succeeding former all-star outfielder Roy "Red" Parnell as manager, he guided the Buckeyes to Cleveland's first championship title. The '45 team won the pennant by fourteen games over the Birmingham Black Barons, the widest margin in league history. The Buckeyes blitzed the Negro American League with a 53-16 record behind Trouppe's brilliant handling of a young pitching staff. They continued their conquest by defeating the powerhouse Homestead Grays of the National League in a shocking four-game sweep of the Negro World Series, beating a team that everybody thought was unbeatable. The Grays had won nine consecutive league pennants and were heavy favorites because of established stars like Josh Gibson, Buck Leonard, Cool Papa Bell, and Ray Brown. The Jefferson brothers, Willie and George, along with Gene Bremer and Frank "Big Pitch" Carswell, made up a strong Buckeye starting rotation. The Cleveland foursome gave up only three runs in thirty-six innings, holding the great Josh Gibson to a paltry .125 average. Meanwhile, Trouppe hit a sizzling .400 and led the team in total bases.

In an interview with writer John B. Holway, Quincy recalled the ease with which they swept the Homestead Grays:

All we had were young guys. [Avelino] Canizares, [Sam] Jethroe. "We going to run you," I told Willie Jefferson. "You're my pitcher." Willie beat them 2-1. The next game we played in League Park [Cleveland]. They had us beat. We tied them up [in the seventh inning]. I got a double and Josh had a passed ball. [Grays Manager] Vic [Harris] walked the bases loaded to pitch to [Gene] Bremer. He hit a double against that high screen in right field to win it [4-2]. The third game in Washington [D.C.] Willie's brother George shut them out on four hits and we won four to nothing. He had so much stuff that nobody could touch him. Happy Chandler was out there looking at the game. The fourth game went to Philadelphia and we won 5-0. Raymond Brown pitched that ball game for the Grays. He was past his prime then. Brown was good back in the thirties—that's when he was really good. I got two hits off his knuckle ball that night. Big Pitch Carswell pitched another four-hitter and we beat them 5-0.

Quincy had total command behind the plate, as his pitching staff held the Grays to a .168 series batting average. That year was one of Trouppe's finest moments.

Future major-league rookie of the year Sam Jethroe, probably the most talented player on the team, remembers, "Quincy pulled us through in '45 to beat the Homestead Grays. He kept us on our toes. You know how players can get sometimes. He kept us focused." Willie Grace, who hit a home run in the Grays-Buckeyes series, recalls the Big Train as "one of the most knowledgeable men about baseball I ever knew," and explains how Quincy, in his role as manager, kept the team, in Jethroe's words, "on our toes":

There was not a better scholar in baseball than Quincy Troupe. You almost had to be a scholar of the game to play for him. He knew baseball inside and out and expected you to know it too. Every year he was there [in Cleveland], we were winners. He lived baseball twenty-four hours a day. We would be riding on the trains some nights, and he would want to have a meeting at two or three o'clock in the morning. Especially if he could get four or five guys together to discuss strategy. Sometimes, we would be riding along in the bus and pull off alongside the road somewhere, at a roadside stop, and if they had a picnic table we would go over there and have a meeting and talk just baseball, all baseball.

With the team we had, we felt like we could beat anybody. In fact, we did . . . the entire season. We didn't have what you would call outstanding stars, we just had good ball players at every position and Quincy's leadership. He was right up on everything that was happening. He didn't miss a trick on the field. Little things you wouldn't think about, Quincy would pick up on everything, all while he was catching and managing. He knew every weakness on a ball club. He was that type of guy.

After winning the Negro World Series in 1945, he joined the American All Stars team in Caracas, Venezuela, with such legends as Roy Campanella, Buck Leonard, Jackie Robinson, Gene Benson, Verdell Mathis, Sam Jethroe, and Roy Welmaker in the lineup.

An equal opportunity manager, Quincy hired the first white player in the Negro Leagues when he signed pitcher Eddie Klepp to a Cleveland Buckeyes contract in 1946, but Klepp failed to survive the season. Local segregation laws in many southern cities prevented him from making field appearances with a black team. That season, the Buckeyes struggled to a 26-27 record. They returned to the throne in 1947 with a 42-23 record to meet the mighty New York Cubans in the World Series. With pitchers Willie and George Jefferson gone, the staff's aces Vibert Clarke and Sad Sam Jones proved to be no match for the bats of Minnie Minoso, Claro Duany, and Silvio Garcia. The Cubans, behind the pitching of Luis Tiant, Sr., and Dave "Impo" Barnhill, beat Quincy's troops four games to one.

After capturing the Negro American League pennant but losing the series, Trouppe managed the Caguas, Puerto Rico, Criollos to a 33-26 record in the 1947-48 winter league. The Criollos defeated Mayaguez in seven games to capture the championship. He was awarded the title of "Honorary Mayor" by the city of Caguas.

After his tremendous success in bringing two league titles to Cleveland, he was hired by the Chicago American Giants in 1948 as manager. The once-powerful American Giants were the league's doormats in 1946 and finished next to last in 1947. Despite Trouppe's best efforts, the American Giants remained in the cellar. Riley Stewart, a pitcher for the '48 Giants, expressed his thoughts about his former manager:

> He was one of the few managers that would fit in in any era. Any era, now or in the past. He was so far ahead in strategy than most managers. I played for [Olan] Jelly Taylor in Memphis and Candy Jim [Taylor] in Chicago and Trouppe was the best manager of the lot. He was a real gentleman. He was clean-cut, and well dressed. He was a model for the guys on the team. He never cussed. He might say "dawg gone." I never played for a finer gentleman. And he knew the game—very well! I respected him more than any manager I ever had. Not even the great Candy Jim was the teacher that Trouppe was.

In 1949, his final year in the Negro Leagues, Quincy joined the New York Cubans as a catcher and assistant coach to tutor Ray Noble, who would later catch for the New York Giants. His winning spirit and influence in the Negro Leagues is reflected by the won-and-lost records of teams he played for. His teams totaled a lifetime winning percentage over 60 percent, good enough to win a pennant in most years.

A typical scouting report on six-foot, three-inch, 215-pound Trouppe might have read: "An excellent receiver . . . Has exceptional knowledge of the game . . . A superior handler of pitchers. He possesses a powerful throwing arm . . . that few base stealers will test. Has average speed on the base paths. Country-boy strong . . . A switch hitter with power from both sides of plate . . . can hit for a high average." Another catcher, Othello "Chico" Renfroe, remembers the switch-hitting Trouppe as hitting prodigious home runs from his right side and line-drive shots from his left side. Renfroe recalls Trouppe as "a demon at the plate, left or right-handed."

He was thirty-nine years old when he finally made his debut in the major leagues on April 30, 1952. Yes, he was twenty years too late. A few days later, on May 3, he caught former teammate Sad Sam Jones, forming the first black battery in the American League. But his catching skills had diminished when Cleveland Indians pitcher and teammate Rapid Bob Feller met him in spring training. Nevertheless, Feller remembers the Big Train as a fellow with "great personality, which made him very likable, and he was very hard working." He adds, "Quincy was a very good receiver. He had an excellent arm, kind of like a Roy Campanella or Gabby Hartnett. He was very good calling pitches and blocked the bad pitches very well."

Rapid Bob also recalls, "As far as a major leaguer, Quincy just came in a little too late because he couldn't get in during his prime. It's a shame because there's no doubt in my mind that he would have been a very good major leaguer if blacks had been allowed into the big leagues when he was in his prime."

Trouppe made only eleven plate appearances in six games, with only one hit, for the Cleveland Indians. After his short stay with the Indians, he was assigned to their Indianapolis minor-league club, where he hit .259 in eighty-four games. Now, at the age of thirty-nine, Trouppe decided to hang up his spikes. The next year, he returned home to St. Louis, where the Cardinals hired him as their first African American scout, a position he held for the next five years. He recommended Vic Powers, Roberto Clemente, Al Smith, Minnie Minoso, and Ernie Banks to the Cardinal organization, but the club declined his advice.

Quincy was let go by the Cardinals in 1957 and soon headed to California to start a new chapter in his life. He married his third wife, Bessie Cullins, in 1964. They became proprietors of a senior citizens' home in Los Angeles, California, called the Queen Anne Manor, where Effa Manley, former Newark Eagle owner, once resided. They also operated a restaurant called the Dugout. After they sold the senior citizens' home, they moved to Hattiesburg, Mississippi, where Bessie preceded him in death in 1988.

Quincy then returned to his roots in St. Louis, Missouri. During the next few years he and I conversed by telephone on a weekly basis, becoming close friends. He enjoyed sharing his baseball travels with me, and I loved hearing about them. He seemed to always have something good to say about the lesser-known, but nonetheless talented, players. He frequently boasted of how Avelino Carnizares was such an outstanding shortstop, Gene Bremer was a tough pitcher in the clutch, and Willie Grace and Parnell Woods were very underrated hitters.

We also talked on several occasions about revising and republishing *20 Years Too Soon*, which he had published himself in 1977 and had since gone out of print. He wanted to leave a legacy; he wanted to leave something that would tell what black baseball was like from a player's perspective. I would be the one to help rewrite it and pull it together. But after many unsuccessful book contracts, the prospects for Quincy's book looked dim. My commitments as Research Director for the newly organized Negro Leagues Baseball Museum in Kansas City, Missouri, were increasing to an unmanageable level, and my volunteer efforts to rewrite his book were gradually put aside. Fortunately, the Missouri Historical Society Press agreed to republish this rare history in 1993, where the editing tasks eventually fell to Tim Fox, in close collaboration with myself and Quincy Troupe, Jr.

This book, though, is only part of his legacy. He was—and still is—nationally known for his extensive photograph and motion picture collection (almost all of the Negro League footage shown in the recent Ken Burns documentary *Baseball* is from Quincy Trouppe's collection). Without a doubt, he was the most prolific photographer of Negro baseball history. He chronicled every event in his lengthy career through photography and film. Today, historians, researchers, film producers, and fans struggle for precious access to this exclusive media chapter in black baseball.

In spite of these achievements as a baseball historian, Trouppe will probably never receive his just due as a baseball player; he will probably never be enshrined in the National Baseball Hall of Fame. Playing in the shadows of celebrity teammates like James "Cool Papa" Bell, Chet Brewer, Ray Brown, Ray Dandridge, Sam "The Jet" Jethroe, Buck Leonard, Leroy "Satchel" Paige, Jackie Robinson, Wilber "Bullet" Rogan, Hilton Smith, Norman "Turkey" Stearnes, George "Mule" Suttles, "Smokey" Joe Williams, and Willie "Devil" Wells tends to ensure one's anonymity. What's more, his published records simply do not reveal Hall of Fame numbers. For example, though he played in eight of the coveted East-West All Star games, the second most of any catcher (Josh Gibson played in eleven), and led his teams to six victories, he batted a humble .200 in fifteen at bats.

However, the true worth of a pure athlete like Quincy is immeasurable. Baseball statistics, be they for hitting or fielding, have qualified barriers; pure genius is unbounded by such narrow guides as a batting average or an RBI total. Quincy stood above the threshold of creative genius. Besides, history should never be reserved for the "great" men and women, and baseball history especially should be all about the people we know and cherish. Quincy T. Trouppe was a man loved by everyone. He was not a flashy, boasting, media-grabbing type of player. According to several players, he never talked much, and he never tried to promote himself. He let his play on the field voice his talents. Another all-star performer, Monte Irvin, sums it up best: "There's one man they never say anything about, a catcher, who was almost as good, or the equal of [Roy] Campanella. That was Quincy Trouppe. Very smart, great arm, good hitter, hit from both sides. When he got his chance [for the major leagues], he was too old." Former teammate Willie Grace adds, "I don't think I ever met a finer gentleman. One thing about him, he would tell you what he thinks, but never in a harsh manner."

Personally, I found Quincy to have a straightforward style, a special closeness with his players, and an uncanny ability to analyze baseball strategy. He possessed low-key confidence and encouraged self-promotion among his players. He was a huge man with an ever-present cherub smile. Quincy's voice was always soft, but it had an authoritative tone, blended with thoughtfulness and tempered with respect.

In Quincy's golden years, he suffered from Alzheimer's disease. I recall sharing some of his grandest moments in black baseball with him on many trips to St. Louis, each trip presenting new challenges as he moved from household to household with me, meeting different sets of relatives. Finally, Quincy settled at the senior citizens' home on Sixty-first and Etzel. Through the years, I watched a man who could turn on a fast ball as quick as anyone become a man unable to turn a spade of dirt with his swollen feet. I watched a man who could remember the batting lineup of every team in the league become a man sometimes unable to remember the security access code to his apartment building. I watched a man who could hold on to a foul tip become a man barely able to hold a spoon and fork. Yes, growing old can be tragic, but you never heard any complaints from Mr. Trouppe. At eighty years plus, he still enjoyed an acrobatic 5-4-3 double play, beautiful women, and the Colonel's original fried chicken, though not necessarily in that order. Despite memory lapses, he always remembered each player's name on every photograph in his massive collection, and he always remembered what batters like Josh, Buck, Cool Papa, and many other legends could, and could not hit, in any count situation. His managerial mind was awesome.

Let's pray that Quincy T. Trouppe will always be remembered for his enduring contributions to our simple game of peanuts and crackerjacks. He was capable of doing great things—when given the opportunity. He brought a passion to the game not seen today. What he got out of it was simply to see his teammates work harder to get better. He played baseball in the style that reflected the intellectual stripping of the game's rules that so dominated black baseball. He emphasized the hit-and-run, double steals, and suicide squeeze plays that became the trademark of the Negro Leagues. He possessed the clairvoyant instinct to know exactly how to win a ball game, whether as a player, manager, or both.

During his twenty years in the crouch position, Quincy's knees were subjected to constant abuse, while foul-tips off his fingers often contributed to his playing hurt. But it was the other teams that felt the pain. According to published statistics, Trouppe batted .311 against Negro League opposition. And in eight years in the Mexican Leagues, he compiled a .304 average. Although an outstanding catcher, manager, and hitter, Quincy never confused fame with success. He always strived to reach the next rung of the recognition ladder.

Quincy Trouppe's homegoing occurred on August 10, 1993, in Creve Coeur, Missouri, a suburb of St. Louis. For me, I will dearly miss the gentleman, the scholar, and the athlete. I will miss the weekly phone calls, the frequent trips to St. Louis, and most of all his infectious personality. No doubt he was a pleasure to see play, because he was a joy to be with.

The Trouppe legacy will be continued by his two sons, the Reverend Timothy Troupe and Quincy Troupe, Jr., a poet and writer. Troupe, Jr., who is best known as the author of the biography of jazz trumpeter Miles Davis, calls his dad "the second greatest catcher of all time. Only Josh Gibson was better, because he was a better batter." He just may be right!

1
From Dublin, Georgia, to St. Louis, Missouri

Mary and Charles Troupe, Mama and Papa to me, raised ten children in a sharecropper's cabin near Dublin, Georgia. I was their youngest child, and as such I had both the good and the bad of being the baby in a large family. Being the baby, I never had to chop wood for the fireplace, our main source of heat in the frosty winters, since this duty fell to my older brothers. I did help with the kindling for the cook stove, which burned hot winter and summer. On the other hand, though my age spared me many of the chores, it also tended to put me under the thumbs of my brothers until I grew big enough to stand up for myself.

Born on Christmas Day, 1912, I had celebrated my tenth birthday before I became acutely aware that the cabin home of my parents, with its love and security, was not the whole world, and that beyond it was a land where everything was divided into black and white, cruelly so. I was just learning that we were a black family in a world where whites dominated.

My Mama was a wonderful person and a fine human being, filled with love for all people, so it hurt her to become aware as her children grew that there were whites in the area who hated us just because we were black. As confrontations became more and more frequent, my parents became more and more concerned.

The racial tension reached the breaking point when my brother Albert, whom we called "Buddy," a boy of spirit, clashed verbally with the overseer of the farm that contracted Papa as a sharecropper. This was real trouble. The overseer came to our cabin and protested to Papa, demanding he take action against Buddy. Papa assured the enraged man that he would handle the problem.

Buddy, whom I worshipped, stood straight-backed and tight-lipped in front of Papa. Although he was only fourteen, he was standing up to the trouble he faced with a dignity that kept his defiance under control. I was seated on the floor near him at the fireplace, warming my back, and I watched him with anxiety. Mama was at the cook stove, but she kept glancing at Papa and Buddy, not interfering but much concerned.

Papa spoke quietly. "Buddy, the overseer says you're a mean boy. He told me you called him very bad names. He wants you punished good."

The firelight cast a rosy light upon the room and shadows flickered over Buddy's face, but they could not hide the spirit in his eyes. "Yes, sir, I expect he wants that."

Papa folded his arms over his chest and asked, "Did you call him bad names?"

"Yes, sir, I guess so."

"Why?"

Buddy looked Papa square in the eye. "Papa, he ordered me to call him 'sir.' And he told me I got to respect him."

The wood in the fireplace crackled, sending off sparks before I heard Papa probe further. "And you won't call him 'sir'? You don't respect the man?"

Buddy replied, "I can't call him 'sir,' Papa, 'cause I don't respect him."

The answer was an honest one, and Papa dealt with it as such. He did not respect the white overseer either, and he knew most of their neighbors did not. The overseer did not like black people, and he enjoyed asserting his authority over them to the point of abuse. Buddy was simply the first individual to challenge the man. It presented a grave problem for Papa.

"All right, son," he told Buddy, "I'll take care of this matter. In the meantime, I'm asking you to stay away from him. Mary and I will decide what must be done."

That night our parents talked for a long time with the kitchen table lamp burning for hours as they sat side-by-side, planning our future. I awoke once when Mama made a pot of fresh coffee. The odor of it filled the little house.

There was a man in St. Louis, a friend of Papa's, who had often written him urging him to come to the big city, get a job, live in a better house, and know freedom. That night Mama and Papa made their decision. They wrote a letter and sent it to St. Louis, inquiring whether a job was still available for Papa.

Coming home in the early evening a few weeks later, Papa brought an answer from his friend. The unopened letter lay beside Papa's dinner plate, for he had decided not to read it until after saying grace at the supper table.

We all watched his face when he finally opened it and read it to himself. He looked from it to Mama, smiling at her. "I have a job waiting for me, Mary, in St. Louis. I'm to leave right away."

Mama's smile was tearful. What it must have meant to her to know that she was to uproot her family and travel to a strange place to begin life in a new way. But she showed us no fear, saying only, "It's a great blessing, Charles."

It was not possible for all of us to go to St. Louis together. Papa would have to work for a time to earn our train fare to the northern city. And he would have to rent a house for us, and that too would take money that would have to come from his earnings.

The problems involved were inconsequential compared to our parents' determination to move us north. They had decided that Buddy's conflict with the overseer held a potential threat to the boy's future, maybe even his life. They knew Buddy's spirited personality could not be brought down by the hated white man, and they feared what might happen between the two of them. There was only one thing to do, and that was to take us away from the situation. The incident with the overseer was just a part of an atmosphere that was growing worse.

Papa decided to take Buddy with him. Then George, one of my other brothers, decided to go along with Papa and Buddy to help out.

In leaving the younger ones of us at home with Mama, it was my oldest brother Phillip upon whom Papa relied for protection and care. Phillip's body had been crippled in his early life, before I was born, when he suffered a fever that resulted in the amputation of a leg. There had been no crippling, however, of his courage or character, and Papa knew Phillip was capable of handling matters at home.

The day Papa, Buddy, and George left for St. Louis, we all got up before dawn for the wagon ride to the train station at Dublin, about twelve miles away. There we gathered in a little family group, suddenly stricken with the tug of farewell and the bleak sound of the engine's whistle. Mama managed to hold off the tears until the train pulled away from the station, but the ache in my throat was too much for me and I burst into sobs. Papa and two of my brothers were gone down the long track, which seemed to stretch into nowhere. Even while I could still see the smoke from the engine, I missed them and wanted them back.

Looking at my mother, I saw that she was crying. My own tears quit as I tried to comfort her. "Don't cry, Mama. We'll see them soon, won't we?"

She pulled me close and I was enveloped in her fragrance, a clean, woodsy, natural kind of perfume created by her cleanliness and her work with the cook stove and fireplace. "Darling," she assured me, "it's just that they ain't never been away from me for more than a couple of days, and they will be so far away this time."

Sad, or not, at the departure of Papa and the boys, we were very hungry when we left the station. Mama decided to get us something to eat and led us to a restaurant, her pocketbook held tightly in her hands. She quickly reviewed the money she had against the probable cost of our meals. We would have to eat lightly, but it would be sufficient until we got home. Phillip and my brother Pal, who was only four years older than I, tagged along behind Mama and me.

We got as far as inside the door of the restaurant and felt the heat and smelled the fried foods. This was the first time I had ever entered a restaurant, and I was delighted, clinging to Mama's hand and taking it all in.

Our entrance caused an immediate disturbance. The diners looked at us in surprise and anger. Some of them laid their knives and forks down hard on their plates, as the exclamation "niggers!" swept the room.

A red-faced waitress nearly dropped a tray as she rushed to get us out the door with the order, "Get out of here! We don't serve no niggers here!"

Mama's hand pressed hard on mine. She started to protest, but she managed to stifle it. She gave Phillip and Pal a quick, warning look, and then without a word she led me out the door while they followed, Phillip nearly stumbling as he walked away on crutches.

Outside, Mama said, "I'm sorry, boys." She reached into her pocketbook, brought out some cash, and handed it to Phillip. "Here, son. Take Quincy with you and go to that grocery store down the street and buy us some bread and cheese. Get some milk, too. We'll eat in the wagon on our way home."

As the wagon jolted over the old country road toward our cabin, Mama told us, "Boys, you know things is pretty bad here now for us. Like in that restaurant. That's why Papa has taken Buddy to St. Louis. He don't want Buddy or any of you to get into any trouble just 'cause you're black. Papa asked me to tell you this: Believe always that he is behind you in everything you do. Believe in yourselves, too." She patted my hand. "And he wants each of you to say a little prayer for all of us every day." She sighed. "We've got to avoid trouble with the mean whites while Papa is gone. You mind that, all of you."

◆ ◆ ◆

During our wait to join Papa in St. Louis we moved to the Ed Darden farm. The Dardens were Papa's friends, and they proved it by easing our lives at that time. There were two Darden daughters; to this day I believe that Maggie Darden was the most beautiful girl I have ever seen.

There were some things that happened while we lived on the Darden place that impressed me—each in its own way. First, I fell in love with a full-breed collie puppy that belonged to the wife of the overseer of the turpentine woods and works, where many of the blacks worked full or part time. The woman knew I wanted that little dog, and one day when he was about two months old she gave him to me.

I named the dog "Wallace" after the only uncle I knew on my father's side of the family, who was such a wonderful person you couldn't help but like him. I always looked forward to seeing Uncle Wallace again, but it never happened.

When I first saw the pup playing in the yard of the overseer's home he was healthy looking, but when I received him I was upset to find he was suffering badly with the mange. I was told to take him to Mama for help.

In her usual efficient and loving way, Mama prepared a mixture for Wallace and brought him to a full recovery in a short time. I loved that dog with all my heart, and we became inseparable.

It was at this time that I earned my first money, and I was awfully proud of being able to help my family. At first, Mama objected to the idea of my working. She told Phillip, who had arranged it through his own employment, that I was too young. "He's only a baby. The work is too hard."

Phillip came through for me. "No, Mama, it really isn't. All he has to do in the turpentine woods is follow me around while I do the tally and put a cup under the little lip in the tree so that fluid can run into it. I'll watch him."

Mama consented and I went to work with my big brother. He kept the scores of each man on the turpentine farm. Every time a tree was chipped, or a cup was hung, the worker called out his number and a mark was placed beside his name on the tally sheet.

Wallace was with me, too, and when my job was done at the end of each day the two of us went rabbit hunting. I was good at it, and often came home with meat for Mama's table.

Then school began and I had to stop working. Pal and I would walk the four miles to the schoolhouse in the company of the Darden sisters. We really had some good times as pupils in that country school.

One Sunday we were all excited waiting for the Dardens to come by and pick us up after Mama had accepted their invitation for us to accompany them to church. When the two-horse Darden rig came to the house to pick us up, we were glad to see they had brought along an eighty-year-old neighbor, who lived alone. We all climbed aboard the wagon and were off to church in our best outfits.

About halfway there we met two white boys on the road. As the wagon started to move past them, they grabbed the old man by one arm and tried to pull him from the seat.

Phillip held on to the old man, shouting out the names of the boys, whom he knew, appealing to them to leave the old fellow alone.

As Mr. Darden stopped the wagon, one of the boys turned to Phillip, who was still calling their names.

"When you use my name put a handle on it!" he said.

"I'll put a handle to your name and when I get through with it you won't need it!" Phillip told them.

Mr. Darden cut in, and even though neither boy was over eighteen years old he called them both "Mister." "Sir! Don't hurt the old man," he pleaded. "We're just on our way to church and we don't mean nobody no harm."

One of the white boys put a restraining hand on his comrade's arm, apparently satisfied with Mr. Darden's remarks. "Next time you niggers won't get off so easy," he said.

Mr. Darden got the horses moving, pulling the wagon away from the whites.

"Lord, I'm so glad it didn't go further," Mama exclaimed. "I know you, Phillip, and I know what you would have tried to do if they hadn't backed down."

Phillip nodded. Even though he was crippled, his arms were much stronger than the average man because of the use of his crutches, but Mama wasn't referring to that. "You're right, Mama," he said. "I had something for them if they jumped me." He slapped his side.

Mama gave him a long look, then said sternly, but not harshly, "You shouldn't be carrying that thing to church. That's very bad."

Phillip did not have to explain to anyone that he needed the security a weapon offered to compensate for his physical inability to defend himself and his family.

Mama pressed her hand to his knee. The Darden wagon traveled on toward the church, but the brightness of the day was gone.

◆ ◆ ◆

Every day, on our way to school, Pal, Maggie, Ida, and I had to pass by a big farmhouse owned by the Smithermans. They were one of the several blacks in the area who owned large farms and had several small houses on their property along with pigpens, barns, a big barn, and a silo.

One day about an hour before school let out we heard several gunshots down the road in the direction of the Smithermans' farm. In a few minutes a wagon came charging past the school with the horses wide open, galloping as fast as they could go.

We all ran to the windows and the door to see what was going on, but we couldn't see who was driving because they were flat on their bellies in the wagon.

"All right, everyone back to your seats," our teacher said after they had passed.

That day, on my way home, I thought about that wagon as we passed the Smithermans' house.

In the evening, Mr. Darden stopped by our house and told my mother about what had happened that day. "Sister Mary," he said to Mama, "I thought I'd stop by to see how you and the boys is doing. How's everything?"

Mama was just beginning to prepare dinner, and she wiped her hands on her apron. "Oh I'm fine Mr. Darden," she said. "You can see what I'm doing. Won't you stay and have dinner with us?"

Mr. Darden moved through the gate up to the porch. "Sister Mary, do you remember those two white boys who tried to molest Old Man King on the wagon the other Sunday when we was on our way to church?"

Mama looked concerned and walked closer to the edge of the porch.

"Hi Quincy," Mr. Darden said to me as I sat on the top step listening to their conversation.

"Sister Mary, keep the boys close for a few days, especially in the late evening. No telling what them white boys might try to do."

"Mr. Darden, did they drive a two-horse wagon with two black horses?" I asked.

"Yes, that seems to describe what Mrs. Smitherman saw very well," Mr. Darden said.

"Mama, we saw them pass the school!" I exclaimed. "They was really running them horses, and laying flat on their bellies in the wagon. We heard some shots a little before the wagon passed the school!"

Mr. Darden looked at Mama and said, in a somewhat cautious tone, "Sister Mary, all of you keep yourself close for the next few days. Oh, we going to be in the right place around this area all right. You all living right here, on the main road; you just have to be careful. Watch out for everything now. And, I'll be seeing you."

It was only a few days later that Mama got a letter from Papa along with our tickets for St. Louis.

FROM DUBLIN, GEORGIA, TO ST. LOUIS, MISSOURI

My joy was tempered with extreme sadness. I was not going to be able to take Wallace.

Grieving, I visited the Darden sisters. Beautiful Ida offered to take my dog as her own. It was a tear-dimmed trail home for me the evening I had to leave Wallace with her. "Be a good boy, Wallace," I told him. "Don't follow me, please."

And I ran from the Darden place, into the evening gloom, as Ida held my dog to keep him from running after me. I could hear him barking as he tried to break loose. I believe I can still hear him barking today.

◆ ◆ ◆

Mr. Darden took us to Dublin to get the train to St. Louis. Mama prepared a lunch basket this time, and we ate on the way to the train.

I had never been on a train in my life, and I was so enthralled with it that I hardly slept at all during the two days and nights of the trip. Our car was up front, just behind the engine. This was the coach for blacks. The other coaches were out of bounds.

Mama had already written to Charles, another of my brothers, who was living in Atlanta. When we arrived in Atlanta, Charles had bought his ticket and was ready.

We all traveled in the same coach.

Soot-covered but thrilled, we arrived in St. Louis. My excitement was high as the train glided past the station and then slowly backed into position on the tracks so the passengers could alight at the platform. It was a long walk from the train to the waiting room, but Papa and Buddy were at the gate and we ran to them and were enclosed in hugs. Papa held Mama close.

"How was the trip?" he asked.

"It was just fine, Charles, but I was so anxious to get here."

Papa put a hand over my head, wobbling it a little. "Quincy, boy, did you enjoy the ride?"

A hug was my answer. I was too happy for words.

We boarded a streetcar to cross town to the house Papa had rented for us in south St. Louis. It was on the levee. It was not much of a house, but Papa told Mama that he would find another place as soon as he and Buddy had worked a little longer at the American Car Foundry. George had gone on to New Jersey to be near my sister Donna, who was married and living there.

◆ ◆ ◆

We didn't have running water in the house, so my brothers and I had to bring water from the lumber yard about a block away. I had to climb up something like a ladder to get over the fence that led to the water faucet.

I got to know one of the boys who lived about thirty-five yards away up the river. His name was Gillis, and his father made clothes props; Gillis's father would row his boat across the river to the Illinois side, where he had found some small young trees. He would cut them down, bring them back to the Missouri side, skin them, trim them, and take them to town to resell.

Gillis and I had a fight one day. I got tagged and picked up my first black eye, but I won the fight. I was fresh from the country, healthy and strong. Once Gillis found out how strong I was, he never wanted to fight again. He became my best friend.

◆ ◆ ◆

School was at half-semester, and Mama said I could wait until the beginning of the new one to start. Before that happened we moved to Compton Hill in central St. Louis. Papa had kept his promise, and we now had an adequate house. Mama was very pleased.

Now all of the Troupe family was in the north; some of the elder children had preceded our leave-taking of Dublin by striking out independently to the east. Eva was in Connecticut; Lee, George, and Donna in New Jersey; and the rest of us, Mama, Papa, Buddy, Pal, Blanche, Charles, Jr., Phillip, and myself, in St. Louis.

I liked the old river city from the first moment I saw it. My life was now full of new sights and sounds. But the old torment of potential and actual conflict between us and whites had not changed much. We had many fights with white boys in the area, especially when I took a newspaper delivery route servicing a white neighborhood.

I learned then to take fighting as part of my job. My paper customers, mostly white, were satisfied with my work, and I needed the money I earned. So fighting my way home to Compton Hill became routine.

The job was very important to me because it helped meet my school costs, including lunch money. It also paid my way into the motion picture theaters.

I was an avid movie fan. Blacks had to be if they wanted to see the shows, since they were subjected to debasement when purchasing theater tickets and segregated from the white audience once inside. Many of the theaters did not allow any blacks at all. When we were allowed to enter, it was only at certain hours of the day and night, and we had to be seated in the area furthest from the screen in a section called "nigger heaven." Despite all this, I went to the movies and enjoyed every moment. No one and nothing could take away what I had earned—the right to laugh and cry at the movies like any other kid.

At this time, Phillip went to work at Leggett and Meyers Tobacco Company, adding to our family income. We were happy with our three-room house and life of relative freedom in the big city.

◆ ◆ ◆

My parents, devout Baptists, held their children in that faith. To this day, not one of us has ever been involved in any kind of crime. There can be no doubt that Mama and Papa did the right thing in moving us north, away from an area where we had little hope of living well. I think my parents were very wise. One of the best things they did was to talk to us, person to person, to help us face our personal problems. And the wisest thing of all that they did was to let us know every day and in every way that they loved all of us. We had no generation gap in our family.

FROM DUBLIN, GEORGIA, TO ST. LOUIS, MISSOURI

They raised us with the high family ideals of love and loyalty and obedience to God. Papa had his own way of interpreting these things for us. I remember one incident that impressed me for life.

Mama had bought a bicycle for Pal, and for a time it was everything to him. Then he became interested in school and girls and the bike was forgotten. So one day, knowing I needed it for my newspaper route, he told me, "Quincy, if you can get Mama to have the bike fixed, you can have it."

I was thrilled. To have a bike was a dream come true. The only thing I had ever owned had been a little wagon I had won in a newspaper contest a long time ago.

The bike needed a new rim for the front wheel, and Mama saved for it. When there was enough spare money in the sugar jar, she had the bike repaired for me.

It became my first love on wheels. I would not ride it to school because I was afraid it would be stolen. I really cherished it.

Then one day Pal and I got into an argument over the bike. He wanted to use it, but I had a ball game to go to and needed the bike for transportation. Besides, I never went anywhere, except to school, without it.

"I'm sorry, Pal," I explained, "but I've got a game on Chouteau Avenue. I'm using my bike."

We carried that argument right into a fight.

Up until that moment I had never gone against Pal because he was older, bigger, and stronger. But now I had grown up to his size, and I was not going to back down any more.

He snatched the handlebars and tried to pull the bike away from me.

I hung on.

Pal was surprised. "Quincy, let go!" he ordered.

"No! I'm going to the game. You let go."

Then, suddenly, he hit me, batting at the side of my head with one hand while holding on to the bike with the other.

We really went at it for a couple of minutes. I had the feeling that he was getting enough, but just as victory loomed for me, he ran over, grabbed an old bike tire, and began flailing away.

Buddy, who was nearby, heard the battle and came hurrying. "Okay," he said, separating us, "that's enough! Cut it out right now!"

I was so angry at Pal for having hit me with the tire that I was crying. My pride was hurt, most of all, and I was ready to go after him again, but Buddy told me to get my bike and go on to the game. With tears of rage pouring, I protested, "He didn't have to hit me with that tire. This is my bike and if I don't want him to ride it, he won't."

Pal seemed ready to tangle with me again, but Buddy held him back. "Don't you hit him again and I mean just that, Pal!"

Pal threw the tire on the ground and ran into the house.

The thing was settled that night at the supper table when Papa took command. I had hastened to tell him what happened. He listened in silence. Then he asked for our moment of thanks to God for what was on our table. When grace was finished, he looked at Pal. "Son, I'd like to hear your side of the story now."

My brother did not hesitate, as I had not. "He started it, Papa. I just wanted to use the bike for a little while to go to the store."

"But you did give him the bike, didn't you? It is Quincy's bike now?"

"Yes, sir. But I only needed it for a few minutes, Papa."

I could see that Papa was not pleased with either of us. He asked me, "Quincy, why couldn't you let him use it? After all, he gave it to you in the first place and that was very generous of him."

"Maybe I would have let him, if he hadn't hit me. That made me pretty mad, Papa."

"Boys," Papa said slowly, "I don't want you to ever forget what I'm going to say. It's this: Don't fight each other. Instead, help each other always. Love one another. Be ready at any time to do what you can for each other." He paused, looking from one to the other of us. "You are brothers. Never forget that."

As Pal and I sat silent, glancing guiltily at one another, Papa turned to Buddy, frowning. "You ought to have stopped that fight before it went as far as it did. Why didn't you?"

Buddy's expression started out solemn, but a smile that was in his eyes crept around to his mouth and became a full grin. "Papa, I'm sorry. But I figured this was Pal's time to learn that Quincy is big enough now to fight him on equal terms. Heck, Papa, for years now Quincy has had to take whatever Pal hands him, but not today. The kid was winning, Papa, until Pal picked up the old tire. That's when I stopped the fight, on the grounds of unfair tactics. But I tell you, Papa, you ought to have seen Quincy! And was Pal surprised!"

Papa's scowl had lightened with each word, and when Buddy finished, they both roared with laughter. Papa's laugh was deep and real, and it set us to laughing, too. Pal and I looked at each other and went off into peals of giggles.

But Papa gave us one more admonition before he closed the subject. "All right, boys, let's take it from here. I don't ever want to hear of you two fighting again. Is that clear?"

Papa got an emphatic "Yes, sir!" from both of us.

2
SCOUTED AT SEVENTEEN

It was really Compton Hill and the friends I had there that brought me into baseball. James "Cool Papa" Bell and Elston Howard, both renowned players, shared an influence on my life.

Bell became one of the all-time great outfielders in the Negro League, while Howard and I chose to be catchers. Our names are well known now all over this hemisphere wherever baseball is played, and we like to claim Compton Hill as our home. I was kind of a link between Bell and Howard since I started playing before Bell retired and played until Howard was well on his way in the game.

My first baseball coach was a lady teacher in elementary school, Miss Harmon. I thought she was the greatest, and she was so pretty.

She started me catching because of my strong arm. No one could steal on me, and we won several banners before I graduated to high school, where catching was my regular position.

When I was just a kid starting to play ball, I spent most of my spare time doing whatever would help develop my body. If I was not playing some kind of action game, I would throw rocks or play catch. My favorite game was played with soda-pop bottle caps. We used the same rules as in cork ball. I think this game had a lot to do with my success in hitting at the beginning of my career.

Playing with soda-bottle caps teaches the first important rule of becoming a good hitter: let your eye follow the ball as it leaves the pitcher's hand. To hit a bottle cap, the batter has to sight it as the pitcher releases it and follow it all the way as it twists and curves in all imaginable directions.

I ate, slept, and breathed baseball. I was thrilled just to see the famous players pass on the street. Whenever Bell walked around, sometimes with his pretty wife, Clara, he was always tagged after by two or three kids, and one of those kids was bound to be me.

Cool Papa Bell was a well-conditioned ball player who managed to keep his weight on an even keel. He was a good-looking man, one of the best dressed in baseball, and it was no wonder he attracted so many young fans eager to walk in his shadow down the streets of Compton Hill.

After I started playing in high school, I got to know Bell and a few of the other players of the St. Louis Stars. During my last year in high school, Cool Papa came to see us play for the city championship.

St. Louis had only two high schools for the colored, so naturally this game was always a pretty hard fought one. The school had arranged for Bill Donaldson to umpire our game.

Donaldson umpired for the St. Louis Stars, and our final game was played at the Stars' park. I had a chance to see some of the players as we were passing the clubhouse on our way to the playing field. They were cleaning their baseball spikes and hanging their uniforms up to dry.

I noticed Cool Papa seated in a box on the first-base line when we went out for our infield practice. He waved at me during the practice, and that made me feel pretty proud. He had let everybody know he recognized me!

The game got started in a professional way. Donaldson came out in his blue suit and really took charge. He said, "All right, fellows, let's have a lot of hustle now," and everyone went into position.

He shouted, "Play!" and the game was on.

Vashon, my school, was home team, so our opponent, Sumner, had first chance at bat. We got Sumner out three up and three down, and in our half of the first inning we got a run on my three-base hit with a man on base. Now, anyone else would have had a home run, as far as I hit that ball, but I was very slow during my high school years.

The St. Louis Stars' park was located across the street from Vashon High School. The grandstand was over half full with my schoolmates, and boy were they cheering like mad when I got my triple.

After our side was out and we went out on the field, I noticed George "Mule" Suttles and Ted Trent in the exit to the grandstand behind home plate. They carried their Stars uniforms in rolls, and they looked like they were on their way to the clubhouse. Fascinated, I watched them as I took my place behind the plate.

Then, around the middle of the game, I saw Ted and Mule had joined Cool Papa to watch us play; as the game progressed, there seemed to be a minor conference going on between umpire Donaldson and Mule Suttles— the consultation seemed to be about me! I don't mind telling you it made me a little nervous, knowing these professionals were in the stand watching every move I made. I sure didn't want to make any bad plays in front of them!

The game went along all right all the way.

Our pitcher, known as Big Blocker, had a fast ball that was just too much for Sumner. We did not have much trouble winning.

That game put the cap on the season of our high school league, and soon the American Legion would start its season. Umpire Donaldson came over to our dugout and talked with Coach Sutton. Following their low-voiced conversation, the coach came over to me and asked if I would like to play American Legion ball. He said Mr. Donaldson was going to coach a team and would like to have me on it.

Boy, that was right up my alley! I had not figured on playing anywhere after the high school league closed.

SCOUTED AT SEVENTEEN

"Peerless" was the name of Mr. Donaldson's team, and we had less than a week to practice before the American Legion League opened its season. We were sponsored by the Tom Powell Post 77, and Mr. Gus Lowe was in charge.

We had a good team; several of us, including Mel Williams and myself, could play more than one position. Mel was a tall, loose, good-hitting first baseman who also would catch when I was pitching. H. W. Grady stood out on defense at second base, and Jessie Askew had the makings of a professional from the start. He could hit consistently with power at the plate, had a good arm, and was a steady fielder. Teddy Corlis was a good fielding shortstop, and Emmett Wilson looked great in center field—he was real fast, could hit with authority, and made some big plays in the outfield. Carl Whitney played right field, had a good arm, and could field and hit. Stanford Buford had a great throwing arm, and Johnnie Edwards, our relief pitcher, whom we called "Mississippi," had a lot of desire for the game. Charlie Hayes was our regular pitcher, and he played outfield also. Charlie could really hit that ball as well as throw, and when he needed help pitching I'd bail him out. Then there was Lawrence Bingley, our mascot, who was great at his job.

On paper, this is how we looked:

Mel Williams, catcher, 1st base
H. W. Grady, 2d base
James Askew, 3d base
Teddy Corlis, shortstop
Emmett Wilson, center field
Carl Whitney, right field
Stanford Buford, left field
Quincy Troupe, pitcher, catcher
Johnnie Edwards, pitcher
Charlie Hayes, pitcher

We had one tough team that we had to beat: the Robins, who were loaded with Theolic Smith, the best pitcher in the American Legion League, William Clay, and Lefty Washington.

Well, we beat them and won the championship in the colored division. Mr. Lowe tried to arrange a city championship play-off between our team and the white American Legion League team champions, sponsored I believe by the Goldman Post 96, but was only able to get them to agree to play us one single exhibition game.

It appeared that the American Legion was pretty much like the major-league teams when it came to playing ball with us. Mr. Donaldson told us that at one time a major-league team had played a black team, but that they had lost so many games that the only way they would play blacks now was in all-star competition.

"Why?" I wanted to know.

"Oh, I guess it was either pride or prestige. The white boys were supposed to be over any black team, and when the black boys beat them it hurt their feelings. Then, too, it was a matter of it getting out to the public, but a lot of people already knew the black boys were just as good."

"Did you ever ump a game between the black and white?" I asked Mr. Donaldson.

He looked at me with a big grin. "Oh, yeah," he said with pleasure, "I umpired behind Bullet Rogan, and the only reason he didn't play the big leagues was because he was black. He was great, and when I say great you can rank him right up there with white pitchers like Lefty Grove, Earnshaw, and Dazzy Vance. Boys, to tell you the truth, I think this is the same reason these white champs don't want to play you, or maybe it's the old heads, the sponsors, who don't want to take the chance. Kids will play anywhere if the game is arranged."

I was pretty excited. I guess we all were. I had been reading about the white American Legion League champions in the *St. Louis Post-Dispatch*. They had a good solid ball club, but I believed we could beat them.

The exhibition contest was limited to four innings, and we played it before the St. Louis Stars–Kansas City Monarchs game one Sunday. Jessie Askew made the big hit that day. The park had a short left field because there was a streetcar shed about 260 feet away standing about 60 feet high, so naturally anything hit on top of the car shed would be a home run. Well, Jessie hit a line drive that soared straight through a door that had been left open in the shed, and that created quite a commotion. During a regular St. Louis Stars game that door was always closed.

Anyway, what happened was that that game, which we wanted to win so badly, ended up in a 3-3 tie.

I picked up some good points from Donaldson that year after I got on as a bat boy with the St. Louis Stars. I learned, too, by watching such players as Bell, Devil Wells, Stringbean Trent, Mule Suttles, T. J. Young, Leroy Matlock, and Dewey Creacy.

◆ ◆ ◆

It was at this time, almost without warning, that we lost Papa in death. He came home one day at noon, complaining that he just did not feel well, but he had no idea what was wrong.

Frightened, Mama called the doctor, and he suggested sending Papa to the hospital at once.

He died there shortly after being admitted.

Mama took it very hard, as we all did, but she was comforted some when all her children came home to be with her during Papa's funeral. I was just sixteen, the only child now living at home with Mama, so now it was just the two of us.

Everyone who suffers the loss of a loved one learns that life goes on, and so when spring came again, I trained every day with the Stars.

During spring training the Louisville Black Caps came to town for an exhibition game. Now the Stars' manager had noticed me throwing the bases, but he already had two experienced catchers, so the first thing that came into his mind was to make a pitcher out of me. He came over and called Ted "Double Duty" Radcliffe. "Duty, I'm going to let this young man start and I want you to catch him."

Radcliffe was a hustler all the way. He could both pitch and catch, which was why he had the name Double Duty, and he was always ready when called on.

Radcliffe took me down to the bullpen and warmed me up. "After you get good and loose I'll give you my target where I want you to throw," he said. "I want you to take a good long stride so that you can get your body behind every pitch. Now, I've been watching you throw the ball. You've got a good arm, and all you need is control. Now just work with me and everything will be all right."

The first two innings I was so nervous I was shaking all over. After walking two men in the second inning, Radcliffe came out to the mound. "Now Quincy, just take it easy and remember everything I told you down in the bullpen," he said. "Keep your eyes on my target. Once you pick up on the target don't take your eyes off of my glove, and make sure you keep plenty on the ball. O.K., you can beat these hamburgers. Let's go."

The Black Caps had such players as Sam Hughes, Felton Snow, Lefty Gisentamer, Anthony Cooper, Joe Scott, Louis English, and Howard Cannon; Cannon had played with the St. Louis Stars a few years back.

Double Duty had many tricks, and his experience really helped. He made lots of batters swing at bad pitches by talking to them indirectly in a conversation directed to me. He would ask me to throw a certain pitch and cross up the batter by moving from one side of the plate to the other. Sometimes he would get out on the outside corner of the plate and call for a fast ball, but his signals to me would be to throw to the inside corner. On other occasions he would stand up and pound his mitt very loudly, his hands almost high enough to touch the batter's elbow, and signal me to throw outside. It was very hard for a batter to guess with him because he hardly ever used the same pattern.

In this game I hit my first home run in professional baseball off left-handed pitching Gisentamer. I also shut out the Black Caps 7-0.

Although I pitched in school and did in this game, my only interest in pitching was to help my team win. I really did not like pitching, but I loved catching.

The next week, while the Stars were still in training, the manager asked me if I would like to join the team as a pitcher.

I said I would like to join the team, but not as a pitcher. I wanted to catch.

The manager said, "Well, Troupe, you have judgment enough to see I already have two very good catchers. It would be almost impossible for you to make the team as a catcher."

"Then, sir, I'll try again next year," I told him, holding to my resolve to become a catcher and not a pitcher.

He walked over, asked me for a fungo bat, and began hitting ground balls to the infield while batting practice was going on. I joined him and started relaying the ball as it returned from the field.

As I tossed the ball to him he said, "Quincy, what are your plans for the summer? Are you intending to play ball?"

"Yes, sir, I practice sometimes with my brother's team. Maybe I'll play regular with him this season."

The manager looked out toward short and made a kind of gesture that he was going to hit the ball on the second-base side. "Quincy, after practice, I'll give you an address in Springfield, Illinois, where you can play every weekend." He turned to me, interrupting himself. "Okay, enough of that. Get a bat and let's see you hit a few."

Trent was throwing practice and on the first ball pitched I hit a line drive back through the middle, carrying Trent's glove a little toward second base.

Wells walked over toward Trent from shortstop, saying, "Bubber, he hit that one like Mule, eh!"

Trent picked up his glove, noticing the webbing had been torn out. "I know one thing," he said, as he turned back to the pitching mound. "He won't get another one down the middle."

The manager came up to stand beside the batting cage. Trent threw one inside and I swung, hitting the ball one hop against the scoreboard, almost four hundred feet from home plate.

Before there was another pitch, the manager came from behind the cage, holding up Trent in the middle of his pitching motion. "Okay," he said, "that's okay for your left, but, you're a switch hitter. Right?"

"Yes, sir, I am."

"All right, hit three or four on your right side," he said, retreating behind the cage.

I changed over to my right side. The first pitch was too close and I had to move back, but on the next I swung, hitting a line drive to left field. The third pitch I drove far up on the streetcar shed.

After I finished hitting, the manager pointed out to left field. "Go to the outfield and catch a few fly balls," he said.

I worked out with Cool Papa, Wilson "Frog" Redus, and Pistol Russell. Bell played center field, Redus left, and Russell right. They explained to me how to throw to the different bases and home plate.

The first throw I made was in the air, all the way to third base. Bell and Russell ran over to me.

"Man, he got an arm!" Cool Papa told Russell.

Russell was the captain of the team, so his remark to me had a dual effect. "Quincy," he said, "you have an excellent arm, but first you must learn how to throw." I was both praised and damned.

"Yeah," agreed Bell, "you see, the way you threw the ball a few minutes ago is not the correct way for an outfielder to throw to the bases. You must throw the ball low so the infielders can handle it, if necessary. Sometimes your throw won't have a chance to get the runner, but if the cutoff man can cut it, he might have a chance at some other base runner. So start your throw low and try to make it reach the point to which you are throwing in one or two bounds. And always throw overhanded."

I thanked them for the tips. The last thing Cool Papa told me that day was, "Quincy, be sure to get your arm good and warm so your muscles will be loose before making a long throw."

That next Saturday I received a letter with a ticket and information on how to get to Springfield, Illinois. I did not have to worry about the trip, however, because Frank Edwards, whom everyone called "Teeny," came by the house to let me know what time we were leaving Sunday morning. Frank was already playing with the Springfield team and knew his way around. We rode up on one of the streetcars, which traveled all the way to Springfield on what was then known as the Inter-Urban line.

I had never been away from home, and it was really a beautiful trip. Mr. John Taylor met me and Teeny at the station. We went to a small restaurant and had something to eat.

That day I met Jimmy Johnson and "Shep," two young players who really showed promise.

We played an all-star team made up of players from the Three I League. I singled to right field my first time at bat, swinging from the left side.

I wasn't too cagie behind the plate. I didn't know too many tricks, and in a couple of innings the Three I League All Stars were out in front. My next time at bat I got hold of one and backed the right fielder against the fence. When I got back to the bench, all the guys gave me encouragement.

The All Stars made two more runs and were out front by three, and that's how it went until the seventh, when I hit one over the right-field fence with two men on to tie the score. We went into the ninth inning still tied up. Then Jimmy Johnson singled to center and stole second base. Jimmy, a track man in school, could really move. This brought up Teeny, who hit a line drive over the shortstop, winning the game.

That spring I kept working with the St. Louis Stars, and they took me on their first trip out of town, landing us in Chicago and Detroit. I got a chance to pitch a few innings in a game during the series in Detroit. Detroit had outstanding men like Jake Dunn, Norman "Turkey" Stearns, and Bobby Robinson, and in the seventh inning I struck out all three. I came up to bat in the next inning and hit a triple to center field.

After I got back home, I learned that Mama had received a letter from my brother Lee, who was then living with his own family in New Jersey. He wanted us to come east for the summer. Mama, however, wanted to think about it before deciding if we would go or not. That left me free to go ahead for a time with plans of my own.

One day, while the St. Louis Stars were playing the Chicago American Giants, Vet McDonald, a pitcher for Chicago, asked me about joining his team. He said they needed a catcher pretty badly. Willie Foster also encouraged me to go, and I finally made up my mind to try it. Mama was still uncertain about the trip east, so she said it was okay for me to go on to Chicago.

When I arrived in the Windy City, the owners had already signed José Maria Fernandez, Sr., a Cuban catcher. Other players among the Giants were Floyd "Jelly" Gardner, John Hines, and James "Sandy" Thompson, outfielders; Harry Jeffries, third base; James Brown, first base; Stanford Jackson, shortstop; Charlie Williams, second base; and now, Fernandez as catcher.

These players were experienced. They could call their shots on the last two pitches in the practice—I remember the catcher calling two shots to right field on a hit-and-run in practice. They knew the principle of swinging late, holding the barrel part of the bat back and pushing the ball to right field. I was just out of high school, never really having had any kind of experience in professional baseball. They were good enough to keep me on for a week.

I returned to St. Louis not too disappointed, because I knew my trouble was that I simply did not have quite enough experience to be a first-string catcher, though I was quite willing to try.

Mama had finally decided to visit New Jersey, and we left St. Louis together, arriving in the eastern city around the middle of the summer. It did not take long for me to drift away from the happy family home in pursuit of baseball. After getting my fill of taking my young niece to the parks, playing tennis and softball, and being generally bored, I wanted to play baseball. So I looked around town for a team. I finally got a tryout with the Newark Browns. I wanted to catch, but again there were already two catchers, so I joined the team as a pitcher. We played a double-header every Sunday. In my first game, I pitched a 9-0 shutout and established myself on the team.

One Sunday, after I had pitched the first game, a baseball scout came down from the stands and asked me if I was interested in playing in the big leagues.

I was amazed at the question. He suggested that I go to a Latin country and learn Spanish, explaining that if I could speak that language I would have a good chance of playing organized ball.

The idea seemed so far fetched to me that to tell you the truth I just did not think much about it at all.

A week before Mama and I left for home, my brother took me to see the Homestead Grays play a major-league all-star team. This was the first time I saw Josh Gibson, Oscar Charleston, Jud Wilson, George Scales, Paul "Country Jake" Stephens, and other outstanding Negro stars from the east; Scales hit a booming home run off of Lefty Fisher that night.

Right after that I got my first chance to play against big-league competition when Joe Stripp, star of the Brooklyn Dodgers, brought his all-star team in to play Newark, and the coach put me in to pitch!

Well, we lost by two runs; Stripp got one hit, a single to center. But I didn't feel too bad about the loss. I still had picked up six wins for the team that summer.

Lee had wanted Mama and me to stay, but because I did not like the east, Mama agreed we would return to St. Louis. We were back home by the end of September, just in time for me to take part in the St. Louis Stars–Homestead Grays post-season game series.

I got a chance in one of the one-sided contests in which Gibson and Wilson hit home runs. This was the first time I saw Gibson demonstrate his power. I thought I had a pretty good fast ball until he hit one of my offerings over four hundred feet to the top of the streetcar shed.

That winter I played basketball at the YMCA. Earning a living was important too, so I took a job in a chemical plant.

Nearly as enthused about basketball as I was about baseball, I got a team together made up of former high school teammates. I really love basketball, and if my personal life had permitted it, I might have followed an opportunity to go into basketball professionally. And even though I was shy, I was dating girls and enjoying a kind of quiet social life.

3
BREAKING INTO NEGRO BASEBALL

In 1931 the St. Louis Stars started their training late in the season, around April, and I got my break when one of the catchers returned to his old team, the Kansas City Monarchs.

But Johnny Reese, the Stars' manager, didn't seem too impressed with my natural ability as a catcher, so I had a talk with Cool Papa; he said he would try to get Johnny to change his mind.

While I waited for a decision, I continued to work out with the team, and finally one afternoon the manager invited me into the Stars' office.

He asked if my parents approved of my playing professional baseball, and I assured him that my mother was enthused. And then, there it was. I was looking at my first professional baseball contract, thanks to Cool Papa Bell. It was really a small one, paying only eighty dollars a month, but I was satisfied and so anxious I did not even finish reading it before signing.

I felt very fortunate playing on a team with so many stars, and when we hit the road for Chicago, Detroit, and Indianapolis, I was really feeling good.

We were on our last stop one Sunday in Indianapolis, on a beautiful hot day, ideal for a baseball game, when I ran into my first rhubarb.

The Indianapolis ABCs had three good rookies on the team, Herman "Jabo" Andrew, Ray Brown, and Tom Parker. I don't know if they felt like I did about it, but it sure was a heck of a game; the second one, I mean. We won the first behind the pitching of Ted Trent, 5-0.

Trent was a big, tall man who could think as well as throw. He would tell me how to be ready to catch certain pitches. I did not understand entirely, being a first-year man. He had two curves—a big one and a small one. The small one is now called a slider.

I had already noticed something unusual that day in the ABCs' Jim Binder, who was the most unorthodox hitter I'd ever seen.

One of the first things I noticed as a catcher while still in high school was that a fast ball was usually hit to the opposite side of the diamond from which a batter was batting, and a curve was usually hit to the same side of the diamond. Well, Binder was a right-handed hitter and he hit everything to right field, regardless of where the ball was thrown. Now that I look back on it, we were in a peculiar situation that day from the start.

The second game wound up going extra innings, and in the twelfth, with two out, the ump called our man safe at first, on a ground ball hit to short, and the man on third scored.

Boy, you talk about argument! You should have seen the beef the ABCs' manager put up on that play.

The fans went wild, throwing seat cushions and chairs onto the field and coming down out of the stands. A couple of chairs just missed Giles and Cool Papa, and they retaliated by throwing them back into the stands. After that, one guy came out on top of the dugout and threw a chair, just missing Cool Papa. This really started a free-for-all. Cool Papa threw his bat, but missed, and big Tubby Barnes went up in the stands after the guy, caught him, and punched him to the floor. I found myself right along behind Barnes, but I didn't get a chance to throw one punch because the big guy had the situation well in hand.

Finally, everything got back in order, but some of the fans made so many threats the police had to escort us out of town.

◆ ◆ ◆

The St. Louis Stars won the championship that year in the American Negro League. We did not have a play-off but we did play a postseason three-game series with Max Carey's white, major-league all stars. Carey's Stars included Paul Waner, Lloyd Waner, Bill Walker, Bill Terry, Heinie Meinie, and Babe Herman.

At the time of this series the Stars' park had the first stationary lighting system in St. Louis, and the first night the Stars beat Max Carey's All Stars 9-8. Trent struck Terry out four times and Herman three out of four.

The Waner boys were the batting heroes of Max Carey's All Stars, but on another night we won 18-2 behind the pitching of Lefty Matlock. Bill Walker, who had the best ERA in the National League that year, started the game and did not retire a single batter!

As for me, I did not get a chance to play in either contest—Reese wouldn't let me in the game. I will never live that down.

The Kansas City Monarchs came to town following the major leaguers, and this time I got a chance to play. I was only up one time, but, with the count at two balls and a strike, I tripled to right field.

Henry "Cream" McHenry was pitching for the Monarchs, and after he got the ball back from the shortstop, he turned, mumbled something, and looked at me. I guess he figured a rookie did not have any business hitting the ball at all against him, not to mention a triple!

We played a couple more postseason game series, and toward the end of the postseason play there was a story in the newspapers that the park was going to be sold to the city. Not only that, but all postseason games were played on percentages, and during our last series with a Cuban outfit, somehow the money was figured wrong. The guys sent me up to the office to get the balance we had coming. I didn't know why they wanted me to go, but up I went, and knocked on the door. Mr. Kent, the owner of the team, opened it and looked at me in a way that brought me to a halt.

"What you want, boy?" he bellowed at me.

"Sir, the fellows asked me to come for the balance you owe us," I managed to get out.

He reached into his desk and came out with a gun. "You young bastard, I'll whip your head flat if you say another word about money!"

I knew then why the guys had sent me up, and made a quick exit.

When the men heard what happened, most walked out, including me. Amateurs were hired to play the final game of the season that Sunday.

◆ ◆ ◆

The park was sold and some of the players went to Cuba. Others took jobs in the city. I went back to work at the chemical plant.

Next spring I received a letter from the Posey brothers in Detroit, who had contacted most of the former Stars about forming a team there. I joined the team at spring training in West Virginia and worked out as an outfielder and catcher.

We played our way back to Detroit, and while we were in Fort Wayne, Indiana, on my first time at bat, I lined a double against the right-field fence.

When I came to bat again a couple innings later, the pitcher took a long pause before delivering the ball; when he threw it, it was shoulder high and just a little behind me.

I froze for a split second before my reflexes took charge and I hit the dirt.

The ball caught me on the meaty part of my wrist, but it sounded like a foul, and that's what the ump called it. I got up pretty riled and headed for first, but the ump stopped me.

"Doggone it, ump," I protested, "the ball hit me on the wrist!" I showed him the place where the ball hit me, but he stuck to his decision. Never one to use profane language, I didn't then, but a few choice foul words raced through my mind.

By now, several of my teammates were out at home plate. Everybody was looking at my wrist—Vic Harris, Willie Wells, Dewey Creacy, and others were really raising hell.

The pitcher who had hit me was just talking nonchalantly to the first baseman out on the mound.

"You son-of-a-bitch, just remember you have to come to bat too!" my partner Bert Hunter said, and Vic Harris burned up the English language threatening to clobber the guy.

Finally, our manager got everybody back into the dugout.

I was still steaming, and I dug in at the plate, getting set.

The pitcher reared back and threw. This time it wasn't aimed at me, and I hit it way out over the left-field fence for a home run.

After that the pitcher wasn't too keen on throwing at me.

The Detroit team had me playing two positions, outfield and catcher. Most of the time I played outfield.

One day Pistol Russell stopped me outside the restaurant where we always ate and said, "Quincy, look in that window. You see that girl behind the counter?" He pointed to make certain that I knew which girl he was talking about.

"Yes, I see her," I admitted, hoping my voice was normal sounding, because the sight of that girl made my heart pound.

"Well, her name is Jackie, and up until this morning I thought I was making time with her. Man," he grinned, "I've been tipping her as much as a quarter a meal. But this morning she didn't wait on me, her sister did. And you know what her sister told me?"

He interrupted himself by indicating he wanted me to take a look through the window at the big, good-looking, brown-skinned woman who sat at a table there with two other people. Apparently they had been observing us, because the good-looking woman had an amused smile on her face.

"Look there," Pistol remarked. "I guess Ethel Waters thinks I'm crazy."

"Who is Ethel Waters?"

He was astounded I did not know who Ethel Waters was. "She's only the greatest entertainer on the stage today, that's all. The others with her are Valaida Snow and one of the Berry Brothers. They're playing at the Michigan Theater."

I gave another glance to Ethel Waters, but my real interest was in the waitress. "What about Jackie?" I asked.

"Well, when her sister told me how she feels, I couldn't eat another bite of that breakfast I paid plenty for, man."

"Why? What did she say? C'mon, Pistol, you haven't told me anything yet."

"Okay, Quincy," he grinned. "It's you she likes. Man, I shouldn't have to tell you!"

I could not say a word. "Me? She likes me?" I thought. All this time I'd been wanting to talk to her, afraid she didn't know I was alive! "Are you sure?" I asked him.

Pistol turned away. "Now you know. Let's see what you do about it."

Well, I got up my nerve and asked her for a date, but she said no.

Boy, was I let down, but she would talk to me a lot about my career and what kind of day I had on the field whenever I came to eat. We were both young, and full of life, and it wasn't long before we had really got to be friends, but she still wouldn't go anywhere with me.

One evening as I was rushing from the hotel to get to the restaurant, my roomie, Hunter, stopped me.

"Wait for me, I'm going to eat too, you big sap sucker."

I waited impatiently while he fooled around with some lotion, and finally he got around to locking the door and we left together.

"Have you got a date with Jackie tonight?"

"Well, I'm not sure, but I'm sure going to ask," I said.

"Man, you got to be rugged. Tell her y'all have a date tonight," he said.

We walked in the restaurant and sat at the counter where Jackie was serving, and when she got the chance she came over. Man, was she looking good.

"Hi, Quincy, how was your day?"

I got my nerve together, looked her straight in the eye, and said, "Honey, anytime a man can have someone as beautiful as you to keep him company, everything has got to be all right."

Jackie smiled.

"You know what, I really had you on my mind today, and I went out there and got four hits in four times at bat, all for you," I said.

Jackie looked at Hunter, who nodded in agreement.

"Oh, Quincy, that's wonderful."

"Yeah, and we really should be having a date tonight."

"Well, Quincy, if you promise me you'll be a good boy, maybe I'll let you take me home."

"Oh, that's a deal. Quincy ain't nothing but a good boy. He ain't never even said a bad word," Hunter said. He was laughing, but that night Jackie did let me escort her home.

She had a small apartment made up of a bedroom and kitchen. She invited me to make myself comfortable, and I did.

Later on, while we were relaxing, we heard someone knocking on the door.

Jackie went to the door and opened it, and there were some white men standing out there.

They turned out to be plainclothes police, and they asked Jackie if she was white, looking at me stretched across the bed. Jackie was very fair, with light-brown hair, like a lot of blacks who look almost white.

Jackie told them she was not white, but they didn't seem to believe her. They wanted to know where she worked and where she was born. She told them she was born in Georgia.

They finally left, and we had the rest of the evening to ourselves.

When I got back to the hotel I saw Russell and another ball player running down the hall into Russell's room, and when I passed by I could hear them laughing.

Just as I reached my room, the door opened and Hunter stood there cursing like crazy, with soap suds all over his head. He could not see who I was because of the suds in his eyes, and he started swinging as I came in the door.

"Hey, man!" I said, sidestepping his big fist. "It's me—Quincy. What happened?"

"Some son-of-a-bitch plastered me with soap," he spluttered. He was wiping the stuff from his eyes with his hands. "If I ever catch up with him, I'll break his goddamn neck."

I couldn't help but laugh, and I pushed him back from the door. "Calm down," I urged, but he got hold of a towel, cleared his eyes, and was still standing there, soaking wet and smarting, when a knock came at the door.

I opened it and Pistol Russell was there, staring at us, straightfaced. "Look," he complained, "you two rookies cut out all that noise up here. What's going on, anyway?"

"Go to hell," Hunter said. "You're probably the son-of-a-bitch who plastered me, and if you are, I'd better not find it out! I'll dart all over hell with your little skinny ass."

"Man, I don't know what you're talking about," Pistol protested. "You woke me up. The fact is, you've got everyone up with your yelling. I just came up here to see what's going on." He really sounded self-righteous.

Hunter told him, "Well, you've seen everything now, so get the hell out of here."

With a smiling glance at me, Pistol turned away from the door and I closed it. "Didn't you see the men before they plastered you?" I asked.

"No. I was asleep when they came into the room. One guy stood at the door to work the light switch while the other threw the suds in my face just as I opened my eyes. The light went off again and they were gone. Oh, hell, you know how they do it."

"Well, I'm sorry," I sympathized, "but maybe you'll be able to get even with them some time."

Everything was going good until midseason, when the younger players started getting promises in place of salaries. Bad news came one day when the manager called us all together and gave the word that our team was to disband. The only good part about it was that he had been able to place all the players on other teams in the league until the close of the season. But it sure hurt my romance with Jackie! Hunter and I were scheduled for Pittsburgh and the Homestead Grays.

Pittsburgh started out being very interesting. One morning in my hotel room I was awakened by a kiss; I opened my eyes to see a young woman looking at the pleased surprise on my face and backing away from the bed. "Oh, my God," she said, "I thought you were Joe Strong!"

I believed her explanation because many people often remarked that Strong and I resembled one another, and I believe he was in the hotel at the time.

I sat up smiling. "Well, don't worry about it. This is a pretty nice way to wake up."

The young woman was very attractive, and when she smiled she was downright beautiful. "I'm Emily," she said.

"I'm Quincy Troupe, from St. Louis. I play for the Homestead Grays, and I know Joe Strong."

After a few more minutes of polite conversation, Emily left. It was a strange meeting that led to a good friendship.

◆ ◆ ◆

Joe Williams was one of the great Negro pitchers of the twenties and even earlier, and at Pittsburgh I had the pleasure of catching him. They said he was fifty-three that season, but his fast ball was better than average, and so was his slider, which we called a curve in those days. He could also throw the sinker. Playing with him was something to remember.

Joe took a liking to me and not a day passed that he did not offer me one of his favorite cigars.

The first time he tried to hand me one, I said, "No, thanks, sir. I don't smoke."

Joe insisted, "Come on! A good cigar will make a man of you."

He smoked only the most expensive cigars and clearly viewed them as treasures. To please him, I finally started taking the things as they were offered. This habit went on all during the time I was with the Homestead Grays.

There was still trouble for some of us in getting our salaries, and I was beginning to feel the pinch. We were all starting to think about contracts with other teams, but we had put so much time in with the Grays it seemed wiser to stay with them and try to collect our back pay.

Traveling from town to town was usually accomplished by piling the team into two or three seven-passenger cars. We were so cramped for space that we organized a kind of Notre Dame shift: when the ride became too uncomfortable, someone would give the signal and we'd all change positions on the rear and jumper seats. We had little time to waste on the road, so it was a rare treat when the cars would stop to let us out to stretch and exercise for a few minutes.

One day an older player who had been with the Kansas City Monarchs the prior year asked Hunter and me if we would like to join that team.

"Should we do it?" I asked Hunter.

"No, I think we might as well stay here. Half the season is gone now, and if we stay we have a better chance of getting our money," Hunter judged.

The veteran player said, "Well, okay, fellows. I'm leaving tomorrow for Chicago to join the Monarchs. If you decide to change your minds, contact the owner there. I'll tell him about you."

We stayed with the Grays for another two weeks, and then I decided to go with the Monarchs. I was so short of cash I had to borrow from Hunter to wire Chicago.

It was money well spent, as it brought me my fare to Chicago within a few days. I traveled from Pittsburgh to Chicago on a bus and checked into the hotel where most of the players were staying.

The team's manager started calling me "kid" immediately. "Hi, kid, are you the boy Frank recommended?"

"Yes, sir. I'm Quincy Troupe."

He was an easygoing fellow, but his knowledge of baseball was businesslike. Scrutinizing me, he advised, "I've got one position open and all I can say is, it's yours if you can make it—left field."

We held our practice at Mills Stadium. The Mills were a very strong semipro team, and they gave us a fit.

I had to beat out an old-timer named Leroy Taylor, who had been with the Monarchs for more than four years. I was learning the strike zone and really rapping on that ball.

In the first game against the Mills, I hit four for four and won the position in left field.

The owner pointed out that the team paid on a percentage basis.

Not surprising to me, Hunter arrived a week later from Pittsburgh and made the team also.

In Chicago, like everyplace else, we were continuously under attack by bedbugs. Most of the hotels where black teams stopped in the big cities and small towns were loaded with bedbugs.

My roomie and I had stayed up many nights in Pittsburgh fighting these monsters until early morning.

We'd look under the mattress, spring, railing, and every part of the bed and find nothing, but as soon as we would turn out the light and get into bed they came full force.

I never did know where these things came from. We were talking about it one day in a hotel lobby, and one of the fellows said that they would form squadrons, crawl directly over your bed, and hide in the ceiling; then they would zoom in on your bed like bombs dropped from planes.

The Monarchs played well over a hundred games during the 1932 season, traveling from the middle west, to Canada, to the southern United States. We had several postseason games with the major-league all stars and the Paul Waner Stars.

There were many towns around the country with very strong teams, like South Bend and Fort Wayne, Indiana. We won more than fifty games in 1932 during the regular season before losing to the Chicago American Giants in Chicago.

Some of those games got pretty hot.

I can remember one game we played that year in a small town in Nebraska one Sunday afternoon. During the game a ground ball was hit to the infield, and on the throw our runner collided with the first baseman. The first baseman really got salty, and several of his teammates ran out on the field trying to cool him down.

He just kept making all kinds of remarks.

"Look, you black son-of-a-bitch," he said, "you're not in Kansas City now and your ass isn't worth two cents out here."

By this time all our players were standing around ready for whatever would start. During the discussion Chet Brewer said something to the first baseman, trying to make peace, and got called a whole string of bad names for his trouble. Now, Chet normally was a peacemaker, but he would hit his own brother when rubbed the wrong way.

"You know, I was just trying to make peace and he called me a black nigger son-of-a-bitch. Just wait till he comes up to bat," Chet said when we were back on the bench.

A couple of innings later this guy came to bat.

The first pitch Chet threw was a big three-quarter-arm curve going away. He followed with a fast ball outside, then cut loose a fast ball shoulder high. The first baseman froze. The ball hit him on the head while he was in a half-stooped position and careened into the grandstand. They took him off the field unconscious. I think having a white owner was the only thing that kept a real free-for-all from busting loose.

◆ ◆ ◆

The season ended in Kansas City. All I had in cash to take home was seventy-five dollars.

When I received that last pay, the owner told me, "I want you to come back next year and hit a thousand." I couldn't help but feel good. My record with the Monarchs that year showed me hitting close to .400, and I knew my name was standing right up there with such players as Willie Wells, Cool Papa Bell, Henry "Newt" Allen, George Giles, Tom Young, Frank Duncan, and Walter "Pep" Joseph. When I arrived back in St. Louis, my brother had arranged to play the Wicks Baseball Club in a postseason game. Terry Moore was playing center field for the Wicks; it was a close game, with us trailing by two runs going into the bottom half of the ninth inning.

Emmett Wilson and Jessie Askew got base hits in succession in front of me, and with the count at two and two, I hit the next pitch deep into left field for a home run to win the game.

This was a game played for no pay, but I really enjoyed it because my beautiful hometown sweetheart, Dorothy Smith, was there to see me play. She and Bessie Tilford almost got mobbed by the crowd of people gathering around to welcome us off the field.

The next season I received a contract from the Chicago American Giants. I was in school at Lincoln University during spring training, so I joined the team later in Indianapolis.

Before I left St. Louis, I tried to get a friend of mine, a young left-handed pitcher named Alfonso Norfolk, to come along with me, but he could not make up his mind. He had everything a pitcher needed to make the grade, so I was sorry to leave him behind.

When I joined the Giants in Indianapolis I was introduced to the manager, Dave Malarcher, known to all the players as "Cap." I felt welcome on the team, and after dressing I went out to the field, where Willie Wells introduced me to my new roommate, Alex Radcliffe.

I have said many times that this was the most outstanding team I ever played on. It included Mule Suttles, Willie Foster, and Ted Trent, in addition to Wells, who was rated the number one shortstop in Negro baseball. Wells did everything extremely well except throw, but he always seemed to know where the ball was going, and he played so shallow that no one could leg out a roller hit his way.

At third base Alex Radcliffe had a great arm, was a good fielder, ran well, and hit hard. He was also very friendly, and that helped.

Walter "Steel Arm" Davis—he earned the nickname during his days as a hard-throwing pitcher—was a little past his peak, but still superb at left field. Norman "Turkey" Stearns was in the same class as Davis, and Nat Rogers, who was also a little over the hill, was having the greatest year of his career in spite of his age. Rogers hit Satchel Paige and everybody else like he owned them in '33.

Larry Brown was one of the greatest receivers of all times; when I say receiver, I mean he was a great catcher. He may not have been the best hitter, or the smartest when it came to working with pitchers, but for receiving, throwing, and catching pop flies, he was tops.

Jack Marshall was a pepper pot with a whole lot of guts at second base, and he was a good team man. Jack was a real kidder, too, and there were members of opposing teams who tried their darndest to spike him, just for the hell of it, but they never did get even with him.

Jack was the biggest eater I ever saw in baseball. It seemed like he just could not get enough to eat at any meal. We finally found a place where the customer was served all he could eat for a certain price, and we figured we had the problem solved. Not so. Jack was charged double because he ate double portions of every order.

Confidence in myself was something I did not lack ordinarily, but these players were established stars and going strong, and I knew I had to prove myself with such a team.

I was the second catcher behind Brown and only played exhibition games and double-headers.

Even so, old-timers still talk about the home run I hit off Satchel Paige in a game we played in Pittsburgh against the Crawfords. That was when Satchel was really fast, too.

My first time up I hit a triple down the left-field line; my next time up I singled to center. Satchel was strictly a fast-ball pitcher in those days. Sometimes he would break off a curve to a right-hand hitter. Being a switch hitter, I was batting left-handed, and he worked more with the fast ball.

My third time up I parked it. There was Satchel, displaying his usual superb control as the count went two balls. The next pitch was a fast ball, knee high, and I swung, hitting it over the top of the right-field bleachers so hard it had bounced off the wall of the hospital next to the playing field before I could reach first base.

Satchel just stood there, watching me circle the bases.

As I came around to touch home I heard a loud voice from the dugout. It was my old buddy and roommate, Hunter. "Hey, I'm pitching tomorrow.

I'll see if you can hit lying on the ground!" he said in his tongue-tied drawl.

That night on Wiley Avenue I ran into Satchel at Crawford's Grill, along with some of the other players. We always had our meals at this popular restaurant, which was owned by Gus Greenlee, the same man who owned the team.

As I walked in the door, one of the fellows sitting at the counter saw me and said, "Hey, Satchel, here's that man."

Satchel, who was standing toward the back talking to a small group, immediately came toward me, smiling. He stopped by Willie Wells.

"Where did you get him?" he asked.

"I raised this boy. He's been playing on the same team with me ever since he got out of high school three years ago," Wells replied.

"Well, he looks like a natural. Oh, yeah, he's a natural," he said to everyone in the room. Then he asked me, "What's your name?"

"Quincy Troupe," I answered in a low, nervous voice.

"Oh, yeah," he said, looking at the others. "I shouldn't ever forget that name after what happened today."

Everyone was laughing as he continued. "I've got a tip for you, Quincy. You can go a long way in this game if you just listen to what the older players tell you. Don't be a know-it-all, take it easy with the girls, and lay off the liquor. I guess you ain't got those habits yet."

When he finished, I told him, "I'm more than grateful and thankful for the advice. I'll always remember it."

From that day on, I have had a certain feeling for Satchel Paige. Without question I consider him to be a great man, and my regard for him is without end.

Well, the next day, to my surprise, the manager put my name in the line-up to catch! This was a happy moment because I really wanted to play against Hunter. He always kidded me about what would happen if he ever pitched against me.

Hunter was a curve-ball pitcher. He had a good fast ball, but his best pitch was his curve. The day before I had gotten three hits off Satch's fast ball, so I figured Hunter would not give me a good fast ball to hit, and my guess was right. The first time up the pitch was an overhand curve. I swung and hit the ball between his legs into center field for a single.

I rounded first but was stopped by the throw to second; returning to the base, I looked over at Hunter as he received the ball from the shortstop.

He rubbed up the ball and walked off the mound a few steps toward first base with a half-grin on his face, saying, "Remember, the game ain't over yet, and don't forget what I told you yesterday."

His threats to throw at me proved to be only kidding. I was up two more times and nothing happened. I suppose I knew it all the time.

The next day we traveled to Indianapolis for a series, and the second day in town the opposing team's catcher came to my hotel room and asked if I would be interested in playing ball in North Dakota. The catcher was Ted "Double Duty" Radcliffe, Alex's brother, who had known me my first year in St. Louis.

I didn't know what to say. I was being treated great in every way, only I wasn't playing regularly.

Ted said, "Well you might do better in North Dakota. There you can get actual catching experience, and they will pay you $175 a month, too."

This definitely put something in my mind to ponder.

"How can I get away from this club?" I asked Ted. "They owe me three weeks' pay."

Ted looked me straight in the eye. "Why don't you just ask your manager, Dave Malarcher, to let you go. He's a real nice guy. Tell him that you would have a chance to play more in North Dakota."

"Do you think he will?"

Ted leaned over and said, "Sure as my name is Ted Radcliffe. I'd go myself only I'm getting more money here. Another thing," he said, "how much are you making now?"

"$140 a month," I replied.

Ted had made his point. I told him I'd think about it and let him know the next day.

I didn't know how to approach my manager, because he really had given me all possible chances, but I finally walked over to the dugout. He was sitting there making out the line-up while the regulars took batting practice.

"Cap, there's something I'd like to do, but first I'd like to know what you think of it."

Looking up, he said, "Yes, Quincy, I'll do my best. What is it?"

"Well, sir, I have an offer to go out to North Dakota for the rest of the season at $175 a month. What's your opinion?"

Cap looked down at the line-up in his hands and back at me. "I don't know, son. How do you know you would like it out there?"

"The main thing is, sir, I'd get a chance to play regular."

Cap looked past me to the other end of the dugout and called to a big left-handed, two-hundred pounder, "Bill, you're pitching today." Then he wrote the name of Foster on the line-up, studied the sheet a few moments, and pasted it on the wall.

"Son, you really would like to go out there, huh?"

Pounding my mitt with my fist, I replied, "You've been swell to me here and I've learned a lot, but I want to be in the game more. I realize how it is here. I want you to understand how I feel."

Cap smiled and stood up to pat me on the shoulder. "Let me contact Mr. Hall in Chicago, and if he okays it, I'll let you know. All right?"

I was soaping myself in the shower after the game when my roommate came in and started tossing questions at me above the roar of the water. "Hey, what happened?" he asked. "Did you talk to Cap?"

"Yeah," I shouted, soap running into my eyes.

"Well, what did he say?"

"Well, he's going to let me know after he talks with Mr. Hall."

"When will that be?"

I reached for a towel and started drying off. "Oh, when we get back to Pittsburgh."

When I was at the mirror combing my hair, Alex came from the shower, wrapping up in a towel. "Hey, buddy, I'll sure hate to see you go. And what are you going to tell your girl—the one across from the YMCA?"

Grinning at Alex's reflection in the mirror, I said, "Well, maybe I'll take a run up here after the season closes. I don't expect to go back to Lincoln this fall."

Alex reached for some hair pomade, saying, "You can drive here in six hours. It's only about 240 miles from St. Louis to Indianapolis."

"I'm not driving. It's the bus, or the train, for me." I pulled on my shirt. "If you see your brother, ask him to send me that address. I'm going to contact his man from Pittsburgh, if Cap says it's okay."

Alex stopped dressing and joked, "You really want to leave me, don't you?"

Buttoning my shirt, I gave Alex a shove on the side of his head and nodded in the direction of Sug Cornelius, who was just finishing dressing, too. "There's ole Sug for a roommate. A real gentleman from down yonder in Dixie."

Alex was always kidding about Sug. He protested, "Oh, no! Don't wish him on me. If I ran around with a guy who owns a nose like that, I'd never get a girl."

Sug Cornelius was a soft-spoken fellow with a very distinctive southern drawl, and he did not appreciate Alex's type of humor. "Look, Alex, leave me out of your conversation."

Alex went over to Sug, who was seated on a dressing stool, and rubbed his head, saying, "Now, pal, you know I was just kidding."

Sug pushed his hand away. "Don't, Alex!" He got up, angry. "I'll show you." He started toward a bat, and Alex ran quickly back to his own dressing stool. Sug shook the bat in his direction. "I'm tired of that stuff! I'll show you, Alex!"

By now the other fellows in the room were laughing, and we all left the clubhouse together. We were all guilty of kidding Sug about his nose, and the angrier he got, the funnier it seemed to us. His shout of "I'll show you, Alex!" was being repeated as we made our exit. All of us were subject at one time or another to unmerciful kidding, and this time it was Sug's turn.

That year the team had bought a new bus, and one week we traveled to play in several small towns before moving back to Pittsburgh for the weekend. We arrived late Friday night, and everyone headed for the sack. But, since there had not been enough rooms available at the hotel that housed the team, the club's secretary and I were given rooms at the home of Gus Greenlee. It was there that I again had a somewhat romantic, and mysterious, encounter with Emily.

Once again I was awakened by her presence as she sat down on the bed while I slept. This good-looking black woman seemed to be developing a habit of appearing at my bedside. It would have been all right if I were in the hotel, but I was a guest in the Greenlee home.

This time I believe she knew whose bed she was sitting on, and she did not want to leave. I had to insist upon it, telling her that she could not visit me like that in a private home. She tried arguing, but I meant it, so she reluctantly gave up her little romantic maneuver and left. When she was gone, I turned over and went back to sleep.

It must have been about fifteen minutes later that Mrs. Greenlee came to my room, knocking loudly on the door. It took only one look at her to see that she was very upset. One of her wrists was bandaged, and she stood there, holding it.

She could not control the tremble in her voice. "Mr. Troupe! I don't usually let anyone stay in my home, ball player or not. Now I want to know what that woman was doing in my house!"

"Mrs. Greenlee," I replied honestly, "I didn't know that young woman was coming here. When I woke up, she was sitting on my bed."

She held her bandaged wrist toward me. "See this? A man came to the door and insisted on coming in. Said his wife was here. That woman, I'd guess. When I refused to let him in, he broke the door glass, cutting my wrist."

At this moment the club secretary came in, and he joined me in apologizing to Mrs. Greenlee. She accepted our embarrassed explanations, but there was a bad moment or two. It would be impossible for me to ever forget Emily.

◆ ◆ ◆

The next day Alex and I went down to the grill for breakfast, and just as we were leaving, Cap came through the door. He called me over and gave me the news.

"Mr. Hall says it's okay and for you to come through Chicago to pick up your pay. Now, son, if you get out there, and don't like it, come right back. You'll always have a job here," Cap promised.

After thanking him for everything, Alex and I left the grill just as Satchel was passing. "Well, every time I look around you guys are here. Don't you ever get tired of this town?" he said.

"The town is all right," I answered, "and I'd like to stick around, but I'm leaving tomorrow."

"What do you mean? We play you tomorrow."

"This ham wants to go out in the sticks to play ball. What do you think, Satch? Don't you think it's foolish?" Alex asked.

Satch pulled his hat off and scratched his head. "Well, maybe he'll be more satisfied playing out there."

"Satch," I explained, "my reason for going out there is that I'd like to play more, and if I stay here, I'm sure to sit on the bench. I played regular last year and had a pretty good season. I'd like to continue that way."

Just as Satch started to comment, one of his teammates passed by. "Hey, Chester! Wait a minute. I'm going that way." Then he turned back to me. "Quincy, if they need a pitcher out there, where you're going, get in touch with me."

Astonished, I replied, "I know you're kidding. Here I am going out to the sticks only because of my lack of experience. I'd be happy right here if I could play regularly."

Satch, hurrying after Chester, flung back over his shoulder, "Just remember what I told you!"

"I'll remember!" I shouted, watching him go down the street. I could not help wondering about his remark. Had I known he was having salary trouble, I would have understood.

Alex and I walked back to the hotel a block away. I made my plans to leave the city by train, wiring to Bismarck for fare; it was in my hands in about four hours.

That evening I went to the park before game time in order to see my old pal, Hunter, who was pitching for the opposing team. I had all my belongings with me so I could catch the train after leaving the park.

Matlock started that night's game for the Pittsburgh Crawfords. A home run by the great long-ball hitter Turkey Stearns in the ninth inning tied the score. I did not get a chance to see all the game, but I heard later that it went fifteen innings and that Stearns hit his second home run to win for Chicago.

It was a pleasant trip to Chicago, and there I found I was certainly expected and everything was in order for me. Mr. Hall paid me for two weeks and told me that he would determine with Cap how many extra days' pay I had coming and mail it to me.

The friends with whom I spent that evening before leaving for Bismarck were very much surprised to learn I was leaving the American Giants. During the course of the evening they learned, too, that I wasn't exactly happy about making my first plane flight.

One of the fellows advised, "You need a stiff highball before going aboard that plane. Take one and you'll sleep most of the way—no worry!"

"I don't drink."

"Well," he insisted, "you don't have to drink to try a highball. It's just water and a little liquor."

"Okay," I agreed, "if it will settle my nerves, I'll try one."

No sooner had I boarded the plane, shortly after midnight, than my apprehension disappeared.

4

CATCHING
SATCHEL PAIGE IN
NORTH DAKOTA

Roosevelt Davis, who had played with the St. Louis Stars the year before I broke into baseball, met me at the airport.

We got my bags together and went into town. Davis took me to the owner of the team, Neil Churchill. He was a big, potbellied man who preferred to stay in the background. He seemed very pleased to have me on the team, and he advised me about hotel arrangements.

When we arrived at the hotel Davis asked me to come to his room as soon as I got settled. About half an hour later I went to see what was on his mind. When I entered his room he was standing in front of the mirror rubbing something that had a very bad odor into his scalp.

Putting my hand to my nose, I asked, "What's that stuff you're using?"

Roosevelt just kept working at his scalp, not turning away from the mirror. "This is dog mange preparation. Seems like my hair is coming out, and I'm using this stuff to stop it." He pointed to a chair by the dresser. "Make yourself comfortable."

Sitting down I asked, "How do you like it, Roosevelt? How strong is baseball out here?"

"I'm doing okay here, Quincy. These people don't know a thing about baseball, except that they want you to win, and that's what I've been doing," he said, looking at me. "Now you're young in the game, so you listen. Catch like I tell you! I only have two signals, and they are up and down. Thumb down means ball breaking down, and thumb up means ball breaking up."

"On the thumb down pitch—is that your curve ball?"

"Look, no curve ball. They are both fast balls. The only thing is that one breaks up and the other breaks down. That's all I'm telling you now, and don't ask any questions. Just catch!"

"That's okay by me. You throw 'em, and I'll catch 'em."

"Now you're talking, buster," Davis said, looking into the mirror again, this time rubbing cream into his face.

After talking to Roosevelt, I went out looking for a movie, but the one playing I had already seen. I ended up in a music shop and bought sheet music of "Moonglow." Two years before, while playing with the Kansas City Monarchs, I had bought a ukulele, and I enjoyed strumming away at it. The music reminded me of Hunter, because he could play a uke better than I, and the fellows always kidded me about it.

About two weeks after I arrived, the team contracted another Negro player, Red Haley. Red played second and first base and could hit the long ball. After adding us to the roster, the other teams in the area became easy pickings.

Haley and I decided to move out of town to room and board with a private family. Mr. Churchill thought it was a splendid idea, especially for me, since I was only nineteen years old.

As the team rounded into form, we ran up one-sided scores against the opposition.

Churchill decided, "Boys, we've got to try to book a few games with stronger teams. The people are on me about it. I've been getting letters, and every time I turn around someone tells me the same thing. Now, I'd like to know if any of you fellows know how to contact teams like the Kansas City Monarchs, House of David, or any other traveling outfit."

Haley spoke up. "Church, I've played with several, and I think I can give you the necessary information." Haley was in his thirties, but played as though he were twenty-five.

Two weeks later the House of David came to town. The House of David was a Jewish traveling ball club, the only one of its kind. They were a well-balanced, experienced team. I did not doubt some of their men could have played organized baseball if the opportunity had been offered. Davis was our pitcher, and he had a registered record of eighteen strikeouts during a game that season.

The game started out smoothly the first two innings, but in the third, the first baseman, an older player in his thirties, came up to the plate.

Davis and I were working like a clock. I gave a signal with my thumb up, but Davis shook me off, which meant the pitch would go down. He went into his wind-up and pitched.

The batter swung, hitting the ball past third, down the left-field line for two bags.

Turning around, Davis looked at the man on second. I saw that Davis was rubbing the ball, then he picked up a bag of rosin, threw it down, and returned to his position. I gave him the "thumb up" signal.

Meantime, the runner on second base was trying to figure out my signals. Davis went into motion and threw. The first pitch was a called strike. The count went to three and two, and the batter struck out. The inning ended on two ground balls to short.

Roosevelt Davis had not gone into details on his up and down pitches, and I soon found out why. Back in those days the Negro League had several pitchers who knew how to use this pitch. It was illegal, but they used it as long as the umpire could not catch them. To work, the pitcher had to be using a new ball, and it had to have been scratched on one side.

If the doctored ball is held with the scratched part down, it will go down, like a screwball, or sinker, but with greater speed. Roosevelt Davis was one of the best scratched-ball pitchers I ever caught.

To doctor the ball, sometimes the pitcher had sandpaper in his glove, on his belt, or concealed some other place the umpire could not find. Sometimes one of the infielders would do the doctoring. I don't know how Davis worked it.

In the sixth inning, the first man up was the center fielder, the House of David's best hitter. The first pitch was a called strike. I gave Davis the "thumb up" sign again. This time the batter swung and missed. He looked out curiously at Davis, stepped out of the batter's box, and picked up a handful of dirt. While rubbing it in his hands, he asked the umpire to look at the ball.

Roosevelt Davis was caught by surprise, and when the umpire asked for the ball, he hesitated a moment, wiping his hands across his forehead and rubbing the ball. The umpire called for the ball a second time.

Roosevelt disgustedly tossed it to me and I handed it to the umpire, who examined it closely. He seemed to approve it and was about to hand it back to me when the batter grabbed it from his hands, saying, "Look, ump! The whole side has been scratched!"

The umpire examined it again, but his expression said that he had probably never seen a scratched ball. Several of the House of David players were hovering around him, and to keep the game going the umpire reached into his pocket and brought out a new ball, handing it to the batter. "Here's a brand new one. Is there anything wrong with it?"

The batter's suspicions were now aroused, and he actually took the ball from the umpire, examined it, and found it had also been marked by scratches. The umpire did not know what to say as he and the players looked at a half-dozen other new balls. They all had the same type of markings.

Mr. Churchill came to see what the argument was about, and the umpire took him off to the side to explain what had happened. Churchill, shaking his head, motioned to the bat boy and told him, "Go to the clubhouse and bring us a new box of balls."

The game got under way again with the new supply of balls, and no one said much more about the incident. Being a youngster, I really did not know what was going on, so when the ump called play, I got down and gave the "thumb up" signal. Davis, however, stepped back off the rubber, called time, and motioned me to the mound.

When I got there, he told me, "One fast ball, and two curves. Understand? I'm not using the thumbs any more."

"Why?" I asked, kicking my shoes in some dirt.

"Look," he interrupted, "you just catch. One fast ball, and two curves."

Pounding my mitt a couple of times, I told him, "Okay," and went back behind the plate.

The first pitch was a line drive to left center for two bases. Up to now the game had been scoreless. The Davids made three in this inning, and went on to make eight more, winning the game 11-2.

In a week or so it got around that Roosevelt Davis had cheated by scratching the ball. Some of the people who had seen what occurred that day were threatening to boycott the park unless Davis was released.

One evening as I was sitting at the dining room table in the boarding house writing a letter to my mother, Mr. Churchill came in. "Hi, Quincy. Is Haley around?"

"No, sir. He drove off just a little while ago in Mr. White's car, but he said he'd be back in about twenty minutes."

Mrs. White, my landlady, came into the room, and Mr. Churchill asked, "How are you, Mrs. White? Are the boys behaving themselves?"

She was a very pleasant woman, and she smiled. "Oh, they are just wonderful. Like my own sons. But I don't understand how Quincy can stay so big and strong, because he doesn't eat at all the way he should for such a big young man."

Mr. Churchill started to leave, but at the door he paused. "Quincy, do you know of a good colored pitcher back east, in the Negro League, that you think would consider playing out here?"

"Well," I replied, "I'm not sure if the guy was kidding, or if he really meant it."

"What guy?" Churchill asked, walking back to the table.

"The day I left Pittsburgh," I told him, "I was talking to Satchel Paige, and when he heard that I was coming out here to play, he said he would come here if the salary was right. I think he's the best pitcher in Negro baseball."

Churchill seemed interested, but a little skeptical. "How much do you think I'd have to pay this fellow Paige?" he asked.

Being young in the game I was in no position to quote salaries, but I gave him a guess. "I think you'd have to pay him around four hundred dollars a month."

Haley came into the room, greeted Churchill, and took a chair across the table from me.

"I was talking to Quincy about obtaining another pitcher," Churchill told Haley. "Since the House of David game, you know, the fans have threatened to boycott until we get rid of Roosevelt Davis. I've got to have another good pitcher, and Quincy tells me we might be able to get Satchel Paige. What do you think of Paige? Do you know him?"

"Satchel Paige! Look, Church, he's the best pitcher in baseball, and I'm not barring the major leagues. But I'll tell you one thing, I don't think he would come out here to play."

Churchill pulled up a chair and sat down. "Quincy tells me Paige is interested."

"Well," I put in, "I'm not certain he meant it, but he told me if my team needed a pitcher to get in touch with him."

Haley shook his head. "I don't doubt Satch told you that, Quincy, but it's hard to believe he would come here."

Churchill was businesslike. "Why don't we send him a wire? Contact him and find out if he is willing to come? I'll pay him the four hundred a month salary. Quincy, do you know where to contact him?"

"Yes, sir, I have the address."

Churchill got up from the table and pushed the chair back into place. "Give it to me. I'll wire him today. Well, thanks, boys. We don't have a game tomorrow, but we will have practice. Mohn will be in charge as I won't be there."

As a personal favor, Mohn worked as business manager for Churchill. He was in the insurance business and did well at it.

Davis got his release the next day. Actually, he was lucky the way things turned out. There was not one word in the newspapers about him, and he was able to get a job with another team.

Haley and I went hunting that day. The game warden had given us permission to kill jack rabbits, and the farmers in the area were glad to get rid of them because they were eating crops throughout the area. I had bought a .22 automatic rifle at one of the hardware stores, and we both enjoyed getting out in the open after those rabbits.

The next morning we went uptown and stopped off at Churchill's office on our way back home. He had a smile on his face a mile long. "Well, boys, I've just received a telegram from Satchel Paige. He's coming to play with us."

Looking surprised, Haley commented, "Boy, still can't figure Satch coming out here."

Handing Haley the telegram, Churchill got up from his desk. "Well, Quincy, you said he was interested. He's accepted the deal I offered. He should be here by Sunday, which is just right because I'll want to run the news in the paper every day through Sunday. I'm expecting a good crowd."

I was as pleased as Churchill. Moving toward the door of the office, which was a part of his automobile agency, I looked through the window to a car on the lot. "Not changing the subject," I grinned, "but how much is that gray sedan out there?"

Churchill came over to stand beside me. "That costs $840, but I could let you have it for $795," he said.

I put my hands into my all-but-empty pockets. "Well, you can't blame a man for wishing. I really can't think of buying a car—I don't make that much all season."

Haley, crossing the room, agreed. "Come on, Quincy, you ain't gonna buy no car." Then he asked, "Church, do we have a game tomorrow?"

"Yes! You know, I got so carried away over this Satch Paige deal that I almost forgot. We're going to Beulah and we'll play the Miners. And don't sell them cheap! They've got a pitcher over there who is a good hitter, too." Churchill gave me a pat on the shoulder as we went to the door. "We'll win," he said. "Don't let them scare you."

"I can say one thing. I'll be up there swinging," I assured him.

We went to Beulah the next day and lost 4-3. Stewart, the pitcher Churchill had mentioned, lived up to expectations. Schafer pitched for Bismarck and turned in a good game, but Stewart spoiled it for him with a home run. That Saturday, Haley, Mr. Churchill, and I went to meet Satch. The train pulled in on time about five o'clock. We made our way through the crowd up to about midpoint. Almost everyone had left the train, and Churchill began to look disappointed as he turned to Haley and started to comment.

My yell brought him to life. "There he is! Hey, Satch!"

We started through the crowd, but there was no losing him in it—he stood six-feet-four, towering over everyone else. I was the first to reach him. "Hi, Satch. For a minute there we thought you had missed the train. You sure had me scared."

"Hey, Troupe," Satch grinned. "Boy, you really told the truth about the sticks. Man, we picked up horses, chickens, everything. And a few miles down the track they waited for a cattle roundup!"

Churchill, smiling from ear to ear, came through the crowd with Haley at his elbow. I introduced them. "Satch, this is Mr. Churchill, the owner of the team. And you know Haley."

Shaking his hand, Churchill told Satch, "We're glad to have you with us. I hope you'll like our little town."

Haley, smiling, also shook hands with Satch. "Boy, I never would have believed this!"

Satch was grinning too. "Well, as I live and breathe. . . . Haley, you old goat! What are you doing out here?"

"Playing ball, Satch, but I never thought I'd see you out here doing the same." Haley was shaking his head.

"Well, I'm here and I'll be here," Satch told us.

The porter brought three bags and put them down on the ground beside Satch. Haley and I each took one and Satch carried the third. We made our way from the station to Churchill's car.

Mrs. White had a room ready for Satchel. After Mr. Churchill left, Haley and I settled down in his room and talked baseball late into the night.

The newspapers had been advertising Satchel Paige as the new pitcher for a week, and our park was jam-packed with fans. There were only two outstanding teams in the area—Bismarck and Jamestown. The Hancock brothers and Barney Brown, a left-handed pitcher, added to the power of the Jamestown outfit, but with Satch on our club, Bismarck was the top draw.

◆ ◆ ◆

After batting practice, the team ran out on the field for infield practice. I took a ball from Schafer and threw to third, starting the exercise. The ball came back to me from first base and I threw it to second base, not noticing who was covering until I had let loose the ball. To my surprise, Satch caught it and whipped it to third like a regular infielder. He took all the rounds and came in with the regulars. The boys got a big kick out of that. Everyone was wondering who was going to pitch, and I came right out and asked Churchill about it.

Church queried, "Satch, are you ready to pitch today?"

Satch looked at Churchill and at the same time reached for a ball. "Oh, yeah. Ready as I'll ever be," he said.

He was ready, too, and we won the game with me behind the plate. Satch really pitched ball that season, winning twelve out of thirteen games. The one game he didn't win wound up a 1-1 tie.

In that game I noticed that Art Hancock was more of an uppercut swinger, and I went out to the mound and told Satch I thought it would be best, though a bit unusual, to throw straight overhand to this batter.

The first time up, Satch had thrown Art a sidearm pitch, and the right fielder had to back up against the fence to catch his drive. The next time at bat he struck out on the overhand pitch.

Hancock came to bat again in the seventh inning, and somehow Satchel must have forgotten about the overhand pitch. Again he threw a sidearm fast ball, on the outside of the plate, and Hancock swung. The ball sailed far out over the right-field fence for a home run, tying the score at 1-1. The game went thirteen innings before darkness ended it.

On one of our free days, Satchel joined Haley and me on a hunting trip. He bought a rifle like mine and told me, "Now, Troupe, I'll show you how to shoot. And we ain't gonna shoot no sitting rabbits, either."

We were all sitting on the back porch of the Whites' house oiling our guns before taking off on the hunt. I told Haley, "Hey, man, tell Satch the truth. I wouldn't like to show him up."

Haley laughed and warned Satch, "Yeah, Satch, the truth is Quincy can shoot, man. And I mean hit a rabbit running seventy-five yards away."

Home for his midday meal, Mr. White drove his car up the driveway just beyond the porch and joined us. "Well, it looks like you boys are going to do some hunting today," he said, grinning.

"Yeah," Satch nodded, "I'm going to give Quincy and Haley their first lesson in shooting rabbits."

"I'd like to go with you, but I have a special job this afternoon." White was a mechanic at one of the big garages uptown.

Mrs. White came to the door and said, "Mr. Haley, Mac just called and said to tell you that the car he told you about has just been sold."

"Doggone the luck. I guess that means we'll have to call everything off," grumbled Haley. The sale of the car left us without transportation.

Mr. White, opening the screen door halfway, turned to Haley. "You boys can take my car if you like. I'll get a ride with a friend of mine across the street."

Since we did not have to leave until Mr. White was ready to return to his job in town, we waited for him to eat his lunch and then dropped him off at his job.

After leaving town, we took the main highway east about ten miles beyond the city limits. I gave Satchel a chance to shoot the first rabbit, which was some fifty yards away. He fired and missed. I aimed my gun, fired, and brought the animal down.

"Say, Haley, this youngster ain't fooling, is he?" Satch was impressed.

"I told you he could shoot," Haley reminded him.

During that summer, Churchill took a '29 Buick sedan as a trade-in on a new Chrysler.

He practically gave the car to Satchel inasmuch as it was his to use, whenever he wanted, and Satch kept it at the boarding house. Churchill wanted to make life as easy as he could in Bismarck for the fabulous pitcher.

One day Mr. Churchill came to me and said, "Quincy, I don't know how to put what I'm going to say to you, but it's about Satchel. You know the fans are really wild about his performance, and so am I, but there is one thing I'd like for you to talk to him about on my behalf. I understand a man has to go out with a woman, but there is a way to do it in any walk of life. Just tell him to be careful about riding white girls around in broad daylight."

This made me think about lots of things concerning whites and blacks. Some whites actually didn't like blacks, and others didn't care, one way or the other, as long as it didn't interfere with them making money. I think this was the type of man Churchill was. He really liked Satchel, and as long as Satchel didn't go so far as to make things bad for Churchill, everything was great.

The season in Bismarck was over all too soon as far as I was concerned, but the time had come to move east for a while. Satchel bought the car he had been loaned and made preparations to drive it back east. Haley and I made the trip with him. We dropped Haley off in Minneapolis, and when Satchel and I arrived in Chicago, the baseball season was still going on.

We stayed in that big city a few days and then I decided to go home.

Satch was going back to Pittsburgh for a few days. "Later on I might go to California," he said.

Winter baseball was still going strong in Los Angeles.

The 1933 World's Fair was in Chicago, but my money was too short to take it all in.

Satchel drove me to the bus station the day I left for home. "Well, Troupe," he said, "keep in touch. You know, I kinda like Bismarck. Maybe I'll go back out there next year."

We shook hands. "Okay Satch. You better write to me first to let me know where you'll be staying. Are you sure about going to L.A.?"

"Almost sure. I'll write you from out there, and if I need a catcher, I'll let you know."

This really perked me up. Satch pulled off. "Be sure to contact me!" I said, watching him drive away.

♦ ♦ ♦

In the spring of 1934 Bismarck was strong in every position except pitching; finally, one day before the season opened, I asked Mr. Churchill if he had heard anything from Satchel Paige.

His face showed concern. "Yes, I heard from him, but I don't think he's going to be with us this year. He's had some trouble with the team he was playing with back there, or maybe he doesn't want to come back this year. He told me something about a left-handed pitcher from St. Louis. Do you know him?"

"If he's the man I think, he's okay," I replied. So Satch wasn't going to pitch for us this year. I pounded my bat on the ground.

"Well," Churchill said gloomily, "if I don't hear from Satchel in the next few days, I'll try to contact the St. Louis man."

We started the season, but everything was a little different from the year before, because of the pitching. Finally Churchill got Lefty Vincent, the left-handed pitcher from St. Louis, and two other pitchers from the Monroe Monarchs came later on in the season. With three fine pitchers, and the local boy Schafer as a good fourth man, Bismarck was able to stay even with Jamestown. They had Double Duty Radcliffe, the player who had recommended me to Bismarck. They also had three other players from the Negro League, Barney Brown, William Perkins, and Sam Thompson, and we never did get past them to remain all alone on top of the standings that year.

Whenever I was away from St. Louis I kept letters going to Mom, as I had grown to call her, knowing she would worry if I didn't. Since I had no desk or writing table in my room, I always used the dining room table, because it was well lit and Mrs. White gave me permission to use it anytime it was not busy.

My landlady had a white girl working for her who did light cleaning and the dishes. She was jailbait age, maybe sixteen, with red hair, a pretty face, and a figure well worth the second look. In addition to that, she was a natural flirt.

One day as I was beginning a letter to Mom, I happened to look up and see the young girl lying on the living room couch, apparently asleep. However, I soon noticed she was noticing me noticing her, and she began to twist, and turn, and move around on that couch making all kinds of motions that sent her dress crawling up over her thighs.

That really took my mind off the letter. In fact, I found myself getting up from the table and going into the living room, where I knelt beside her on the couch. When I did that she opened her big blue eyes and gave me their full effect, so I kissed her hard, square on the mouth, and she returned my kiss eagerly.

"Quincy, don't," she whispered, "Mrs. White will see us." But she made no effort to move away, and her dress remained high on her thighs. I found myself kissing her again. After that she didn't say anything.

I don't know what it was that stopped me—whether it was her age, or the different races we belonged to, or simply where we were.

Whatever it was caused me to abruptly pull away from her embrace, stand up, and pull her dress down. "Look, be more careful," I said. "You shouldn't do this to any man."

She smiled, sat up, patted her hair into place, got up, and went into the kitchen, flipping one last look back at me with those blue eyes.

I admit it was not easy, but I did sit back down at the table and finish the letter to my mother.

I was able to write Mama often about the outstanding season I was enjoying. In fact, our whole team was playing at the top of our form, and Hilton Smith really rounded out and developed into a pitcher to be reckoned with.

The Chicago American Giants came out to play a series of games in Bismarck against our team consolidated with Jamestown, Valley City, Fargo, Grand Fork, and three teams from cities in Canada.

Our consolidated team broke even in the series, part of which was played in Canada. I really enjoyed the trip, which left me with a lasting appreciation for that beautiful northern land.

At the end of the season I returned home and started playing basketball and volleyball at the YMCA, same as always. Once again I received offers for the coming season, and the best came from the Kansas City Monarchs. So I took a quick trip to Kansas City and signed the deal. The owner made certain he would have me as a player by buying me a new Ford, which I drove home proud as I could be.

◆ ◆ ◆

Spring training was held in Marshall, Texas, and the manager and another player drove with me to join the club. Training was hard, but the environment was pleasant, because we trained on the campus of Wiley College.

While we were training, the K.C. Monarchs received information on several young ball players in Monroe, Louisiana. Three of them were brought to our camp: Eldridge Mayweather, a first baseman; Robert Madison, a pitcher; and Willard Brown, a shortstop.

Brown looked real good from the start. He was a right-handed hitter who showed exceptional power to all fields, but he did not have that power arm from deep short behind third base. His hands, while good, were not sure. The manager, Sam Crawford, saw this and after a while sent Brown to the outfield.

It was at this time that Willard Brown found his position. To see him walking to and from the field, one would think he was very slow, but this guy could jet when he wanted to run.

Brown is the one who challenged the feats of Josh Gibson. He was like Gibson in some respects. He could hit the ball out of the park, but swung at a lot of bad pitches, whereas Gibson did not. Who knows? Brown may have been as great, or greater, than Gibson, if he had been a little more patient and waited for strikes. He could hit a bad ball, but frequently went at pitches he couldn't reach with a ten-foot pole.

Then there was Henry Milton, who started his career with the Monarchs that year also, but tragically died at a very young age from spinal meningitis.

When training ended, and the team broke camp, we played several games on our way north through Texas, Oklahoma, and Kansas.

One day I had trouble with the manager in a game against the House of David because he wanted to call pitches from the bench that were in conflict with the way I saw things.

Chet Brewer, an outstanding curve-ball pitcher, started this game, and the first hitter grounded out to short. The next hitter swung on a first pitch, a curve ball, and Milton made a great catch against the left-field fence. After about three innings that same hitter came to bat with two men on. This time another pitcher was in the game for the Monarchs, a pitcher who did not have much of a curve and only an average fast ball.

I decided a fast ball would be the best pitch to make this batter hit. The count was two and two, and the manager yelled from the dugout, giving me the curve-ball sign. I called for a fast ball instead, and the batter hit a weak pop fly that resulted in an easy out, retiring their side.

When I reached the dugout, the manager asked what kind of a pitch the batter hit; when he found out it was a fast ball, he went wild.

That did it for me. When we got to Wichita, I decided to leave the team.

The owner of the Monarchs talked to me for hours trying to get me to stay, but my decision was made. I left the next day.

It took me two days to reach Bismarck, which was rough, because I had never driven any distance by myself before. A defective gear gave me some trouble on the road, but it wasn't serious. I finally got there after some exasperating delays.

Besides a raise in salary, Mr. Churchill had good news for me—Satchel Paige was coming. There was no doubt about it. He had a telegram saying Satch would be in Bismarck within the next two days.

We had all our previous players back from the previous season, and now we would have Satchel, too.

Look out Jamestown!

That team actually contacted Chicago to sign Willie Foster just to pitch one game against Satch, and in that game Satch knocked in all our runs and we beat them 3-2.

That year Satchel bought another car from Churchill. Coming back from a little trip to Winnipeg, Canada, in my car, Satchel began to ride me about how cheaply my car was built in comparison to his. As I was driving along, engrossed in his joking, I missed a curve sign; the next thing I knew we were in a sharp turn my car couldn't handle at the speed we were traveling. We skidded into a ditch on the side of the road and bounced back onto the road into the other bend of the "S" curve. When we made it through that, I stopped the car.

Barney Morris opened the door on his side in the back and fell out, rolling into the ditch, yelling, "Oh! Oh! Lord!"

I bolted out of the driver's seat, ran around back, and slid into the ditch beside Barney.

He was sitting there in the damp dirt holding his stomach as though he were in pain.

I knelt beside him, anxious.

There were tears in his eyes as he looked up at me, but there was something else on his face, something I never suspected—he was convulsed with laughter.

"Hey, what's wrong with you?" I asked.

He pointed toward the front door of the car where Satchel was just emerging, and roared anew. "Oh, Lord! I've never seen anything like that—that big man getting down on the floor rolling into a ball. Man, what a sight!" He was enjoying every minute of it, but then in an afterthought cut himself short. "You better see if Satch is all right," he said.

Haley and Smith were out of the car, standing on the lip of the ditch, looking down at us. Haley asked, "What's wrong?"

Satchel came to the ditch, too, and told Barney, "Look, I don't know what you're laughing about, but whatever it is, it ain't funny!" Then Satch gave me the full measure of his steady gaze. "Look heah, Troupe, if you can't drive this jalopy no better than this, you better let me take over."

Before I answered, I got out of the ditch, went to the car, and saw it was undamaged. I pulled a few weeds out of the grill, and then told Satch, "Man, I admit I missed the curve sign. But whose fault was it?"

"Okay, Troupe, if you promise not to miss another curve sign, I won't say another word to you between here and Bismarck."

"Well, just to put everybody at ease, I'll let Haley drive from here on in."

That relaxed everybody, including myself, and in a little while we were all asleep except the driver. When I woke up, Haley was entering the driveway of the house where we roomed in Bismarck.

It wasn't long after my return to the White home that I found that the beautiful but unrestrained girl with the shining auburn hair and very white skin still had me on her mind.

Why take a chance with jailbait? The statutory rape laws were still on the books. I left her strictly alone.

We had a series of games with the Kansas City Monarchs who had, as usual, one of the best black teams in the league.

Charlie Beverly was pitching for them. He was left-handed and had a fast ball that smoked. My second time up I caught one, hit it against the center-field fence, and rounded the bases before the ball could be returned to home plate.

Kansas City also had two of the fastest men in the Negro League, George Giles and Eddie "Pee Wee" Dwight. I felt pretty good throwing out both as they attempted to steal second base.

I got to know Satch pretty well. As his teammate and friend, I soon learned he could clown one moment and become deadly serious the next. His complex personality made him immensely interesting.

Satch was on the slim side, physically, but he enjoyed a challenge and we always jousted on the playing field. Satch figured he could box, and he always picked on me as his sparring partner. One day while clowning around I grabbed him. Man, was I happy to let him go! I was six-foot-three and weighed about fifteen pounds more than Satchel, but he was mighty powerful.

That day I realized why Satchel's fast ball was so deceptive. He had long, wiry arms. His stride was long also, and with his long, strong fingers he could put such tremendous back spin on his fast ball that it would rise two to four inches while traveling from his hand to the batter. This is why his fast ball looked like a marble to the batter, and I think most players who hit against Satch would agree.

Any player who has had experience in pro or semipro baseball knows a knuckle ball sometimes looks so big coming up to home plate you can almost see the seams. Satchel's backspin really deceived players about the speed of the ball. When I was catching Satch in 1933 and 1935 he really had it. When he got off a fast ball, the hitter could hardly ever even foul it.

Umpiring in the Negro League was pretty bad, and most good hitters learned how to hit the high pitch, because the umps called a lot of high pitches strikes. You had to learn how to overhand high pitches, or you would not hit much.

In organized ball you can wait for a good ball and take your cut. So most players in organized ball become accustomed to swinging level, or a little up under the ball.

If you tried that with Satch you were in trouble. If you swung under the ball you had no success, and if you swung too level, you just hit a big fly ball, or a high pop up.

◆ ◆ ◆

During the season, Churchill found out about a tournament in Wichita, Kansas. He made arrangements to play in it, and this included our using the Kansas City Monarchs' best pitcher, Chet Brewer.

Churchill could be a wizard at the bargaining table.

He scheduled a few other games for us on the way down to Wichita, and the first of these was played in Pierre, South Dakota.

I will never forget that one.

In the seventh inning, we had a 2-0 lead and Red Haley, playing first and up to his usual practical jokes, got word to everybody to surprise Satchel with a sit-down strike around the mound if we still had a two-run lead going into the bottom of the ninth.

The score held. Satch seldom talked much about pitching, but he loved to talk about his hitting, and as we went out onto the field to take our positions, he kidded me about the line shot he hit his last time up, which almost took the pitcher's glove to center field. The ball had been returned by the second baseman, who forced a man at second for the final out.

After Satch finished his warm-up, I threw the ball to second. Satch turned as usual to receive the ball from the third baseman, but what he got instead of the ball was a picture of the whole team sitting on the ground behind the mound.

Satch just stood there, absolutely confounded. "Say, now, looka heah! What's goin' on?"

The guys really broke up laughing, and Red Haley told him, "We're on a sit-down strike."

Satch turned and walked back to the rubber, commenting, "Well, ain't this somethin'."

I went out to the mound and the third baseman came running in to toss the ball to Satch. "We decided to let you and Quincy finish this inning," he said.

Satchel did not seem too pleased. He said to me as I started back behind the plate, "Say, Troupe. I ain't goin' to try to fool any of those guys. So you know what to expect."

Satch wasn't kidding, either. He reared back and fired.

The first batter swung, missing, then took the next pitch with his bat still cocked in the air.

Satch made a wind-up that seemed to put the batter in a tense position, like a man trying to fight his way out of a trance. And, boy, did Satch throw a fast ball! Again the batter swung and missed, strike three.

The next man, I guess, wanted to make sure of getting in all three swings, as Satch threw him three fast balls and he took his cut at all of them.

The next guy approached the batter's box cautiously, peered out, and choked up on the bat a little in order to get a piece of the ball and avoid striking out. He even managed to foul the first pitch, but that was as close as he got. Satch made his famous wind-up, and on the next pitch the batter swung after I already had the ball in my mitt.

During my first year playing in St. Louis I had learned lots of tricks, and I tried one now. The batter was choking the bat even more to avoid striking out. Satch had said he was going to throw all fast balls, so I called to him. "Well, Satch," I told him, "I see he is choking up. For this last pitch, let's see if he can reach a curve with that short bat." I gave Satch a target on the outside corner, and the hitter, being a right-hander, was really expecting the curve. I gave Satch the fast-ball signal.

The pitch came belt high, about two inches on the outside corner for a called strike three. You should have seen the other team's faces. Satch had thrown nine pitches and the game was over.

CATCHING SATCHEL PAIGE IN NORTH DAKOTA

All the fellows crowded around congratulating Satch on his feat. "Say, now, looka heah. I don't want none of this stuff you done here today when we get to Wichita," Satch said straight-faced. Then he grinned.

◆ ◆ ◆

One night during the tournament, Smith and I decided to go out early to see one of the other games, and we just happened to sit behind two scouts who did not know we were players. One of them observed, "You know, there are a couple of good black players in this tournament."

"Yeah, but you know the problem with recommending a Negro to the club."

"Well, so many players are from Dixie, and it would be pretty hard for them to fit in with the colored boys."

"Aw, I don't know. I don't think that would make a lot of difference if the front office would ever actually sign one up."

We couldn't see all of the game because we were coming up next and had to go down to the locker room and suit up.

"Smitty, you're from Louisiana," I said. "What do you think of what those scouts were saying about southern ball players?"

"Troupe, I've come up playing with white boys, and I really believe the southerners understand blacks better than most northerners. I think some southern people wanna hold to that old tradition, but most are really good at heart."

"Look, man," I pointed out, "things are changing every day, and that goes for tradition. But maybe it won't happen overnight."

"Well, it wouldn't affect the majors, anyway, because all those teams are located in cities above the Mason-Dixon line."

"Yeah, Smitty, but you know by the time a change does come I'll be too old to throw the ball back to the pitcher."

Leary, our shortstop, one of nine white boys on our team, pulled up a stool next to me and started undressing.

"Hey, Quincy, what's this about you getting old? Boy, don't rush it. You'll get old fast enough," he said. Leary was from a small town in Montana.

"Well, what do you think, Leary? Do you think any Negro players will ever get into the majors?"

"Gosh, Quincy, that's a pretty hard question. I think eventually someone will get up the nerve, like Churchill, and hire both blacks and whites in the major leagues."

"Do you think they could play together the same as we do on this team?"

"Why not? Think of the opportunity that will be afforded both sides. Quincy, I'm almost sure it will work whenever someone gets the nerve to try it."

Churchill stuck his head in the door and spoke in a quick, snappy voice. "All right, fellows, hustle it up. Our game starts in forty-five minutes."

Bismarck swept the tournament with seven straight wins, and Brewer,

Satch, and I were selected on the all-tournament team.

This is probably where the breakthrough for blacks into the major leagues originated. There had been mixed teams in colleges for years, but the opening of the Wichita tournament, with a mixed team, really put the idea on organized baseball owners' minds.

◆ ◆ ◆

Taking advantage of our popularity, Churchill made arrangements to play the Kansas City Monarchs, who were big favorites in Wichita.

Barney Morris started for us, and the Monarchs won a very close game.

Satchel and Brewer had been advertised to duel against each other, and we moved on to Kansas City for this final game.

I had been playing center field in all the tournament games, with Ted "Double Duty" Radcliffe doing the catching, but when Churchill made up the lineup for that night game in Kansas City, he had me catching and Satchel pitching.

We jumped right on Brewer for three runs in the first inning.

I got real satisfaction out of this game, even though I twisted my knee swinging at a low, inside curve ball and had to leave the game. Bismarck clobbered the Monarchs, 8-3.

Then we were off to Denver to play the House of David, who had won the Denver post-tournament championship.

The rivalry was keen, and all the newspapers carried Satch's picture with a story stating he was the outstanding pitcher in the Wichita Tournament.

We cleaned out the House of David and moved on to Omaha for our final game of the season. After it was over, Churchill paid off the players, wished them luck, and said, "I'm looking forward to seeing all you boys back next season."

Satchel and I finished the season with the Kansas City Monarchs, who signed us up to play against the Dean brothers' all-star team.

People are still talking about the Dean boys, and I have often been asked which was the better pitcher. In my opinion, Dizzy was tops. I am not taking anything away from Paul, but Dizzy had the know-how, confidence, control, and everything else a pitcher needs. I've never met a pitcher I couldn't hit, but there's one game against Dizzy I'll always remember.

We were playing in Oklahoma City. Paul started the game, and Dizzy finished it. I had a double off Paul in two times at bat, and grounded out my first time up on Dizzy. Now on my last time at bat, with the count at two and two, I was keyed up and really ready to take my cut. Dizzy served me up one of the best change-of-speed balls possible. I watched it go by for a called strike three.

Quincy's parents, Charles and Mary Troupe. Courtesy Quincy Troupe, Jr.

The Troupe family moved to St. Louis around 1922, and the St. Louis Stars quickly became Quincy's heroes. They are shown here after winning the 1928 Negro League World Series against the Chicago American Giants. Ted Trent, George "Mule" Suttles, and James "Cool Papa" Bell, all on this team, played important roles in getting Quincy's baseball career started in St. Louis. Courtesy Normal "Tweed" Webb.

20 YEARS TOO SOON

Quincy's first break into professional ball was with the St. Louis Stars. After that team broke up in 1932, Quincy played over a hundred games with the Kansas City Monarchs. His roommate and good friend Bert Hunter is second from the left. Left to right: Newt Joseph, infielder; Bertrum Hunter, pitcher; Newt Allen, infielder; Frank Duncan, catcher; George Giles, first baseman; Quincy Troupe, outfielder; Chester Brewer, pitcher; T. J. Young, catcher; Muchie Harris, outfielder; Charlie Beverly, pitcher; Carrol "Dink" Mothell, infielder and manager; Cool Papa Bell, outfielder; Willie "Devil" Wells, infielder. Courtesy Quincy Troupe, Jr.

Facing: Quincy attended Lincoln University in Jefferson City, Missouri, for a time in the early 1930s before signing on with the Chicago American Giants. This photograph, which shows him on the Lincoln campus, is inscribed "From me (Quincy) to you (Dorothy), Lincoln University, 1932." Dorothy Smith was his high school sweetheart. Courtesy Quincy Troupe, Jr.

20 YEARS TOO SOON

Quincy loved playing the ukulele, even though Bert Hunter was better than he at it, much to the amusement of their teammates. Courtesy Quincy Troupe, Jr.

In 1933 Quincy left the Chicago American Giants to play with the Bismarck, North Dakota, Cubs. After the Cubs' pitcher, Roosevelt Davis, was let go, Quincy suggested inviting Satchel Paige to come out and pitch for the team. To everyone's surprise, he did. Back row, left to right: Hilton Smith, Red Haley, Barney Morris, Satchel Paige, Moose Johnson, Quincy Troupe, Ted "Double Duty" Radcliffe. Front row, left to right: Joe Desiderato, Al Leary, Neil Churchill (owner), Dan Oberholzer, Ed Hendee. Courtesy Negro Leagues Baseball Museum, Kansas City.

Baseball was only one of Quincy Troupe's athletic interests. This photo, taken during the 1936 AAU Tournament of Champions, shows Quincy the boxer delivering a knockout blow to Yancey Smith. Years later Quincy's friend Archie Moore would tell him that he was too nice to be a professional fighter. Courtesy St. Louis Mercantile Library Association.

In 1938 Quincy proposed to Dorothy Smith. This photo of the couple ran above their wedding announcement in a St. Louis newspaper. Courtesy Quincy Troupe, Jr.

5
GETTING STARTED IN THE MEXICAN AND PUERTO RICAN LEAGUES

At home during the off-season in '35, I played some basketball, but St. Louis had started its first Golden Gloves tournament. All the guys at the YMCA kept urging me to enter, so I finally decided to give it a try.

I won the local championship and went to Chicago for the Midwest tournament, where I won three bouts and lost one.

Back home, I KO'd Belleville, Illinois, Golden Gloves champion Art Boschert in the first round of the first mixed amateur bout ever held in Missouri. I went on to the national tournament in Providence, Rhode Island. After winning four straight victories, Governor Green presented me with the heavyweight trophy cup honoring me as champion.

One evening during that period of Golden Gloves competition, while sitting downstairs in the locker room waiting to be called up, Joe Louis came in to greet us. I don't know about the other fighters, but I had a kind of humble feeling. Here was this great pro, wishing us well and taking the time and trouble to encourage us, when we were not even good amateurs yet.

Louis spoke to each of us. It was the highlight of my life at that time.

He was a great fighter, world-famous, and above all clean-cut in every respect. He really looked the part of a champ, which he was.

That same year Archie Moore and several other amateur boxers, including me, went to Cleveland to participate in a tournament. Archie and I reached the semifinals before losing on decisions. Lem Franklin was the winner in the heavyweight division.

One night in Cleveland I went with Archie and some of my other teammates to visit a friend I had met there while playing baseball with the St. Louis Stars. I had been considering getting into professional boxing, but the talk about baseball that evening helped me to make up my mind. It was no contest. My love for baseball was just too great to be denied, so the spring of '36 found me returning to Bismarck.

The year before, Jessie Askew had made his debut in professional baseball with the Clay Brook Tigers. He had a good year, and I tried to interest him in going to Bismarck, but he had just married—an elephant with a steel chain could not have pulled him away from St. Louis.

The team was as strong as ever, but without Satchel Paige. Satch returned to Pittsburgh and later went off to the Dominican Republic for the remainder of the season.

A lot of outstanding players went to the Dominican Republic to play that summer.

We had another good season, with Hilton Smith getting a chance to show his ability.

In anticipation of tournament competition, Churchill started making plans. He contacted the Chicago American Giants and made arrangements to use Ted Trent.

We entered the 1936 Wichita tournament, and Smith continued his excellent year by establishing a tournament record that still stands: thirty-six scoreless innings. The year before Hilton had not gotten a chance to play a single game. Satch won four games and Chet three, but this time Hilton pitched four games without allowing a score.

It was a good year for me again. My base running and all-around play got me back on the all-tournament team.

In my first time at bat in the tournament, I batted on my right side against a left-handed pitcher and struck out. My next time up, I decided to hit on my left side because of the short right-field fence. Well, the first pitch on my left side was an inside fast ball, and I hit it over the light tower in right field for the longest home run in the tournament.

The catcher came over with the pitcher and asked me what kind of ball I hit. I told them it was an inside corner fast ball.

The catcher turned to the pitcher. "I told you it was an inside fast ball!" he said.

Hilton Smith and I were the only Negroes on the all-tournament team that year.

The day after the tournament was over, we went downtown, where our owner was staying, to turn in our uniforms and receive our salary.

Just as we entered the hotel lobby, Mr. Dumont, the tournament organizer, called us to the side. "Boys, I was talking to a couple of scouts yesterday at the park, and what do you suppose one said to me?"

Hilton looked at me, puzzled.

"What, Mr. Dumont? Are they interested in signing someone off our club? You know, two years ago Louisville signed a first baseman who had been playing with us," I said.

The tournament director replied quickly. "Oh, they're interested in someone on your team, all right. This scout said he would recommend paying $100,000 each, for you two boys, if you were white!"

"Well, sir, we're available right now," I said. "I'm sure you've noticed that color doesn't make any difference on our club."

"Sorry, fellows," he replied, walking away. "I just thought you'd like to know what the scouts think of you as ball players."

So, in a scout's opinion I was worth $100,000! And yet that opinion was totally worthless to me because of the color of my skin. Being the leading hitter on the Bismarck team from 1933-36, hitting over .350 each year, didn't mean a thing as far as the major leagues were concerned.

After the tournament, Smith and I joined the Kansas City Monarchs again to finish out the season.

We had several postseason games with the major-league all-stars. I could hit those guys like I owned them, and they knew better than to try and steal on me.

That fall I returned home again, and for one year I stayed out of baseball.

Then in 1937, working as a salesman for a milk company, I soon realized I was looking forward to my hours off the job to play baseball, especially on Sundays at Tandy Park.

Police officer Thomas Brooks had charge of a team that played there; he would pick me up after work and drive me to the park. Officer Brooks played semipro ball, and he was a very good curve-ball hitter. He could have played professional ball.

There were some big questions in my life that got answered in '38. First of all, I had been going with Dorothy in St. Louis for years, and the time had definitely come to do something about it. Then there was the injury to my right shoulder, which I picked up while boxing in '37. Somehow I had to work out how all this was going to tie in with the strong tide of baseball pulling me toward the new season right around the corner.

Well, I got in touch with Mountain Drop Mitchel, manager of the Mound Blues team in Illinois, which was also known as the Indianapolis ABCs, and we got together on a contract.

Then, one evening, while standing in our favorite place in the hallway, I asked Dorothy to marry me.

"You'll have to ask Mama if it is all right," Dorothy said. She was very happy, and our kiss was really something to remember.

"Oh, honey," I told her, "I'm going to do that right now."

Maybe no mother is ever surprised when a man asks for the hand of her daughter. I can say that Mrs. Smith seemed to know I was ready to pop the question.

"Yes, Quincy, it's all right. You have my consent and blessing," she said, almost before I got the last word out of my mouth.

I couldn't say anything for a moment. "Oh, thank you Mrs. Smith," I finally managed to say. "I love Dorothy. I'll take good care of her, and make her happy."

I walked back into the hallway without saying a word.

Dorothy looked at me and I opened my arms.

She came running. "Oh, Quincy. I'll be a good wife to you," she said.

Holding her quietly, I spoke our plans. "Honey, get Bessie for a witness, and we'll go to City Hall tomorrow and get married."

◆ ◆ ◆

Dorothy was so glowing and lovely that anyone could tell we'd just gotten married. We only had a short time together before I had to leave for spring training, and we made plans for her to join me in a few weeks.

I started the season for the Mound Blues playing outfield, because a catcher has to have a good throwing arm, and at this point I could hardly throw back to the pitcher.

That year I found out that throwing the ball for distance really helps the arm gain strength, and after a while the soreness went away.

The trouble with my shoulder didn't affect my hitting at all. To tell you the truth, I really laid wood to that ball and had an outstanding year. This was my first year back in the Negro League since '33, and I hit way over .300, along with teammate Ted Strong.

The fans voiced their sentiments through the Chicago Defender by voting Ted and me into the East-West all-star game in Chicago, where I played left field for the West.

I really played inspired ball that year, and my reason why walked in the door of the team owner's club one day as I was sitting in a booth with John Lyles, telling him how much I missed my bride.

"There's Dorothy now," John said, grinning.

I was convinced John was kidding, but I looked around anyway and Dorothy was there! I had been expecting her, but not so soon. You should have seen me running across that room.

We embraced and the fellows crowded around. My little wife was so sweet and beautiful, it took me awhile to let her come up for air.

"Fellows," I said, introducing her to them all, "this is my wife, Dorothy. We've just been married, and now we're going to make up for lost time."

Dorothy was friendly and popular, and I was so very proud of her. Her visit was not long, but we enjoyed every moment.

After the baseball season was over, Ted tried to get me interested in playing basketball with the Harlem Globetrotters, but that meant spending more time away from my wife. I declined the offer.

◆ ◆ ◆

During the winter of 1938-39 I ran into Cool Papa Bell, who was playing in the Mexican League, and we talked about old times. I told him about the outstanding year I had and my participation in the East-West game.

"If they need a catcher, be sure and let me know," I said.

I worked for one of the big steel companies during the winter, and it really kept me in condition. It was the hardest job I've ever had. I had to fork slag out of the pit into a big steel pan after hot steel had run into the ladle, and place chains around the ears of the molds after the red-hot steel had been poured into them. I used a burlap sack around my legs and waist to ward off the heat.

I made it through winter, and one day in March I received a letter to report for spring training.

Now I had to figure out which was the best thing to do—play baseball or stay on my job? My wife was pregnant, and I had to be sure how she felt.

One evening, after getting home from work, she had one of those great soul dinners waiting for me—greens, black-eyed peas, neck bones, corn bread, the works. Usually, for just the two of us, she didn't put on too much of a spread. "Honey, I know you have to feed two, but why all of this tonight?" I said jokingly.

She took a glancing look at me and said, "Darling, I know you would like to return to baseball, because that is part of your life. You see honey, you won't be getting this kind of food on the road, so I decided to fix you something special tonight."

Preparing my plate, I walked over to her and said, "Honey, I love you, and you are really a wonderful wife to understand how I feel about baseball."

She turned around to face me, with tears in her eyes, and put her arms around my neck. "Darling," she said, "after all, a woman must keep her man happy and well-fed. I'll miss you so much this year—not being able to visit you now, with the baby coming."

I held her for a long time. Finally, we sat down and ate dinner.

After giving my company a proper notice, I collected all my pay and a leave of absence. I made all the other necessary preparations and was off to spring training.

I really didn't want to leave my wife, but this is a part of baseball.

With mixed emotions, I sat on the bus and moved out toward Mound, Illinois, with a feeling inside that was the greatest of all. My wife wanted me to play baseball.

◆ ◆ ◆

While I was in spring training I got a wire from the Carta Blanca team in Monterrey, Mexico. Cool Papa had told them about me, and they made an offer.

I went to St. Louis and discussed it with Dorothy. Then I was on my way to Monterrey.

The owner of the team had asked me to bring a pitcher, and the only man I could persuade to go with me was Eugene Smith, a native St. Louisan. Eugene's mound work was not outstanding, but he hit the ball with so much authority that the manager decided to play him in the outfield.

To my surprise there was a player on the team who blamed me for bringing him bad luck in the past.

The player was Roosevelt Davis, who I had caught in Bismarck when I first broke into that league.

We started talking about old times, and it soon became clear he really regarded me as a bad omen, showing up once again to jinx his career.

Roosevelt was doing the same thing in Mexico he had done in Bismarck, throwing a real mean emery ball that was giving batters a fit. He was pretty cocky about his success in the Mexican League, and one day when we were losing a game by eight runs this attitude got him into trouble.

At the top half of the eighth, the manager wanted Davis to go in as relief, but he refused. In the bottom half of the eighth, we made nine runs and went into the lead. Then Davis started telling the manager he was ready to play. However, the manager put in another pitcher, and we won the game by one run.

Following this incident Davis was released from the club.

Once again, he wanted to blame me for losing his job, but, just as in Bismarck, the fault was all his own.

After the season was one month old, the owner asked me to find a couple of pitchers for the team. I talked to Eugene, and he told me about Willie Jefferson and Eugene Bremer, both of whom were playing with the Memphis Red Sox. I wrote to them about playing in Mexico, and in a week I got a letter back saying they would come if the deal was right.

The owner made arrangements for me to leave for Memphis right away to pick them up. He also advised me that two of the team's stockholders would accompany me to the States.

When we arrived in eastern Texas, we decided to stop in a small town to get dinner. We walked into a restaurant and sat down at a table near the door.

We sat there a long time. I noticed people looking at us, and one man, on entering the place, stared so hard at us that he stumbled over another customer at a table next to ours.

Finally, a waitress came over and said, loudly enough for everyone to hear, "We can serve you two, but not him." Her pencil was pointing at me.

"Why can't you serve him?" one of my Mexican friends asked.

"Mister, I don't have to tell you why. We just don't serve niggers here."

My second companion told her very quietly, "Well, if we can't all be served here, none of us will be." He rose to his feet.

The waitress was blank-faced as we left the table. "That's okay by me," she said.

On many occasions during that trip, we had to make out on unheated meals. We would have really been up against it without grocery stores.

In West Memphis, Arkansas, we were parked near an intersection about fifty yards from a service station waiting for Willie and Eugene to come by with their traveling gear. After we had been waiting about forty-five minutes, a police car pulled up and asked what we were doing. My comrades did not speak English well, so I got out of the car and approached the officer. "We're waiting for some friends to meet us here in a few minutes," I said.

He hardly gave me a chance to finish. "Look, black boy. You can't wait around here. So let the highway hit you where the little dog bit you!"

By some turn of luck, as I was walking back to the car, Willie and Eugene pulled up in a taxi, and we all left together.

There are a lot of ignorant white people in the south and also in the north, but I believe most white Americans actually want to do the right thing. I was concerned about my Mexican friends seeing how some whites act toward blacks in America, but I am afraid they already knew.

The team was out of town when we arrived back in Mexico, so we had a light workout every day. After the workout our reception was just like after a game. The park stayed half-full, and the onlookers came forward to ask for autographs when we were coming off the field.

Of those two pitchers I brought back from the States, Willie Jefferson proved to be the better one. The manager used Eugene Bremer in the outfield more than in pitching since he was very fast and a fair hitter.

It was an interesting year. Most of the non-Mexican players were from Cuba. They were experienced and had also played in the Negro League.

I played ball with the greatest Mexican ball player of that decade, Epitario "La Mala" Torres. He was scouted by several major-league scouts, but he refused to play for an American team; he was a very dark-skinned Mexican and well aware of the color problem in the United States.

One day the Monterrey team made a trip to Texas. We entered the U.S. through Brownsville, Texas.

When we entered the immigration office a big, red-faced man sitting behind the first desk hollered, "Take off those hats!" I was not wearing one, but a lot of players were. I am certain nineteen-year-old La Mala, who was playing with us at the time, received a very poor impression of Texas hospitality.

Later on that afternoon we decided to go to a movie, but we were barred because we did not come during the time set aside for blacks to go into the theater.

As I've said, La Mala never signed to play ball in America, probably because of such incidents of prejudice. But with his ability to do everything well—his good hitting, fielding, running, and throwing—he was Mexico's gain. The majors lost a great one.

I was both proud and sad to travel through America with him, but I wanted him to see as much of my country as I was seeing of his.

Word of my first son's birth came from my mother-in-law and reached me at my hotel in Mexico. I was one proud man, but full of regret for being away from Dorothy and our son, whom she had named Quincy, Jr. It seemed as though our marriage was becoming a perpetual string of hellos and good-byes. Being away from Dorothy was getting to be a bad habit. I was aching to be by her side, but there were so many miles between us. I sat down and wrote her a long letter telling her how proud I was of our growing family.

The first year in Mexico ended well enough for me. The record shows I hit over .300.

In 1940 I drove to Monterrey, Mexico, with Dorothy, Quincy, Jr., and Theolic Smith in a car I had bought that winter that I was anxious to put on the road.

We left from St. Louis, and I stayed behind the wheel for a thousand miles until we reached Palestine, Texas. There I pulled over to the side of the road and asked Theolic to take over.

He looked at me, surprised. He giggled and said, "Oh, man, I can't drive."

"You mean to tell me that you can't drive a car?"

Smitty was still laughing. "I didn't tell you I could drive before we left home, did I?"

After I thought about it I realized he had not.

Although I loved to drive on the highway, I was exhausted, but there was nothing to do but accept the situation. Neither Dorothy nor Theolic could drive. So I settled down in the front seat and slept until the sun rose.

When I awoke, I let Dorothy and the baby stay asleep in the back seat, while Theolic sat beside me, calling out a warning on all coming curves in the road. We motored on toward Mexico.

Theolic was recognized as one of the best pitchers in the Mexican League by the custom officers at Laredo, and we talked baseball awhile before going on into Monterrey, from which Theolic took the train to Mexico City.

The year was going great. For once during the baseball season our family was together, and I was in excellent condition mentally and physically, really playing ball. Some of my most interesting days occurred playing against my buddy Theolic.

Then Dorothy and the baby became ill. We were not certain why, but we figured either the food or water was not suited for them. We waited awhile for things to get better, but their condition only worsened. I really became alarmed, and made arrangements for them to return to St. Louis. It was very hard for us to separate. We were back on that hello–good-bye routine, and my beautiful Dorothy was pregnant again.

Some months later, Dorothy gave birth to another son, Timothy. I received the news through a telegram from my mother-in-law while I was still winding up the baseball season in Mexico.

I bought a box of cigars and passed them out to everyone I knew in the hotel. Martin Dihigo took my cigar and invited me to have a drink. I really did not care about drinking, but he would have interpreted my refusal as an insult, so we went to the hotel bar and I let him buy me a beer.

We talked about old-timers, and I asked him about John Henry Lloyd. "How would you compare him as a shortstop to Willie Wells, Dick Lundy, or Doby Moore?"

"Lloyd," he stated, "was the greatest of them all." He sipped his drink, smiled, and told me, "We called him 'Cuchada,' which, in Spanish, means 'spoon chin.' He had a long chin and talked very slowly in a high-pitched voice. Sometimes a pitcher would think he had him set up for a pitch, make his best effort, and Cuchada would hit a shot for a base hit. When he reached first, his high voice would laughingly taunt, 'You thought you had me, eh? Well, you can't fool the old man!' He was then about thirty-seven years old."

He also told me Chino Smith was one of the greatest hitters he ever saw. When Adolfo Luque was in his prime, pitching for the Cincinnati Reds and the New York Giants, he had one of the best curve balls in the big leagues. But when he faced Chino, in Havana, Chino would spit at his first two strikes as they went by and then come through by lining a shot for a hit.

◆ ◆ ◆

In 1941 I took Leslie "Chin" Green to Mexico with me. We had been raised together in St. Louis, but somehow he and I always ended up playing on opposite teams. Chin had a great year in Mexico, hitting around .360 and finishing second in the league. I felt pretty proud, because I was responsible for him playing in Mexico.

During my first two years in the Mexican League, I hit .300, but I did not get off to a good start in '41.

Still, one day the owner of the team called us in for a meeting and held me up for praise. He had received information that some players were breaking training. At the meeting, he stressed the importance of players keeping in good condition. He used me as an example of an excellent player who stuck by the rules, and noted my popularity with the Mexican fans; he even said he would let me break training if he thought it could make me a better player.

That same year, Sam Bankhead played shortstop for Monterrey. He was the most outstanding of the Bankhead brothers, and he could do everything exceptionally well. Although his weakest point was hitting, his season's average was always .300.

One day at the office, as we were receiving our pay, Sam happened to see my check.

"Hey, man, what's the matter? Have you been drawing? Do you owe them money?"

Surprised, I replied, "No, I don't owe the club anything. Why?"

Sam did not answer right away. We walked up to the corner of the main street and waited for a taxi. "Quincy, this isn't any of my business," he said as we stood there, "but may I ask what your salary is per month?"

"I don't mind saying, Sam. It's $175 a month and expenses."

Sam shook his head. "Quincy, you should make more than that. You're a real good ball player. You can do everything well, and boy, I'm telling you, while you still really got it, make them pay you. I believe you don't know how really good you are."

A taxi stopped, and we were on our way to Hotel Bridges. All through that ride I was thinking about what Sam had said. As we walked through the lobby of the hotel, a couple of youngsters came over and asked for autographs. We signed them and went into the restaurant for lunch.

When we were seated at a table, I asked Sam, "What should I do? You see, I've already signed a contract for this year."

Sam ordered a bottle of beer, settled back in his chair, and relaxed. "If I were you, Quincy, I'd go to the manager. Just tell him you want more money.

He knows your ability, and I'm sure he could get you a raise quicker than anyone else."

That afternoon the manager and I had a talk at the park, but we did not reach any agreement. After the game he came over to the end of the dugout where I was changing my baseball shoes. "Quincy, I talked to Señor Ferrara about you. He wants to see you in his office at ten in the morning."

I gave my baseball shoes and mitt to the bat boy, who delivered them to the hotel every day after the game. "I'll be there, Chile," I told the manager.

He nodded. "The owner thinks a lot of you, Quincy. So don't worry. Everything will turn out all right."

I did get a substantial raise, and I earned it. My play won raves the rest of the season.

The task was not easy. That year, Josh Gibson, Ray Dandridge, Willie Wells, Leon Day, and other black stars were in the Mexican League.

Gibson was the greatest hitter I ever encountered. I played against him in three different countries, and he did something great in each one to solidify his stature.

Almost everyone who speaks of Josh will agree with me on how well he could hit, but they often forget the rest of his game. Josh Gibson was not just a great hitter. He was also a smart ball player with a good arm, a big man who could run and catch. He had confidence. He simply believed he could hit anybody, and he could. Babe Ruth had the same problem as Josh—I understand Babe was a very good outfielder, but he is certainly best remembered for the sixty home runs he hit during a single season.

During one game, Monterrey against Veracruz, the ump called a strike on Josh on a curve that was a little outside the plate. I wished he hadn't, because that really got Josh hot.

Now anytime you made Josh mad you had a problem. If that wasn't bad enough, I also was having trouble with our pitcher. I wanted him to show Josh the curve and make him hit a low fast ball going away, but he shook my sign off. The curve he threw came over the middle of the plate, and Gibson swung, meeting the ball solid. It took off like a jet, hitting a sign on top of the second fence in center field, quite a distance behind the first fence, 420 feet away from the plate.

My battery mate was really shook. In the dugout, when the inning was over, I told him, "Look, Echeverria, don't let that inning bother you. Gibson will hit any pitcher who can throw the ball. You see, we pitch outside, and if it isn't down on his knees he'll hit the ball over the opposite fence. If you pitch inside it must also be down on his knees, or he'll hit the ball over the left-field fence. So, you see, the percentage is to pitch low, but sometimes you will get it up unintentionally, just as you did the last inning. Now that guy Dandridge, in their lineup, is almost as bad as Gibson. Only he hasn't the power. So bear down on 'em. Keep something extra on that ball."

Many Cuban stars played in the Mexican League—Martin Dihigo, Ramon

Bragana, Silvio Garcia, Augustin Bejerano, Santo Amaro, Hector Rodriguez, Alejandro "Home Run" Crespo, and Pedro Page. When the season ended I formed, and managed, an all-star team, and we toured the United States, winning all ten games we played.

The team looked like this:

Josh Gibson, catcher
Quincy Troupe, 1st base
Ray Dandridge, 2d base
Buzz Clarkson, 3d base
Willie Jefferson, pitcher
Leroy Matlock, pitcher
Barney Brown, pitcher
Johnny "Schoolboy" Taylor, pitcher
Cool Papa Bell, center field
Sam Bankhead, right field
Leslie Green, left field
Willie "Devil" Wells, shortstop

The Jones brothers from Chicago wanted to sponsor us, but the president of the Negro National League blocked the plan; each of the players was once the property of a team in the Negro National League and had to be reinstated and returned to their former teams. So we disbanded in Chicago, and most of the players headed south to play in the winter league.

Before going to Puerto Rico, I returned to St. Louis. Dorothy was not at all happy that I was about to take off for another country and would be gone for a long time again. I did not like leaving her and the children, but it seemed to me, at that time, that I had no other choice.

I was in St. Louis a week. While I was there Jessie Askew told me about Doc Bracken, a young pitcher. I went to see Doc in an exhibition game, and he turned out to be much like Jessie had said: he had a really live fast ball, a sharp curve, excellent control, and the poise of a veteran pitcher. The only thing he lacked was experience.

I tried to get him interested in playing professional ball, but his reaction was the same as Jessie's: "Baseball does not offer enough security to go into professionally."

While I was still home the Kansas City Monarchs came into town and played Bob Feller's All Stars, with Satchel Paige pitching for the Monarchs.

The manager wanted to use me in the game, but the owner said he couldn't, because all players who performed in Mexico were temporarily suspended.

It was the 1941-42 season, and I went on to Puerto Rico. After three weeks of idleness, I faced Leon Day, a fast-ball pitcher, and on my first two times at bat I struck out.

The club owners were sitting on the dugout bench, not saying anything, just looking. I really started to concentrate and did manage to get two hits before the game was over.

Gibson burned up the league. He told me one day when we were playing their team, "Troupe, I'm not swinging for home runs. I'm going to try to hit .500." Looking at him, I could see he was serious.

"Man," I replied, "you don't have to swing for home runs. With your power, if you get a good piece of it, it'll go out anytime, anywhere."

That afternoon he was just meeting the ball and driving it through the infield like a shot.

One morning, news of Pearl Harbor being bombed came during a game in Guayama. A lot of changes were soon made in Puerto Rico. There were blackouts. Fortifications and airstrips were hastily constructed. Anti-aircraft guns were set up.

And on a personal level, there was something else—my wife's letters were no longer full of warm expressions and enthusiasm.

We continued to play, traveling from town to town under blackout conditions. At certain hours of the night, the entire island was without lights. In Aquadilla and Mayaquez, Perucho Cepeda and Menchin would sit on the fender of the car and guide us home.

We played good ball despite the war. Barney Brown, my left-handed pitching battery mate, received the most valuable player award at the end of the season, winning fifteen games. Monte Irvin, Bill Byrd, Roy "Campy" Campanella, Bill Wright, and Lennie Pearson also made their mark in Puerto Rico that year.

I first really noticed Irvin in a game we played in Guayama, when he went back to the scoreboard in right center and caught a drive off Perucho Cepeda's bat. Perucho was one of the top Puerto Rican hitters in the league.

Two innings later Monte caught a fly ball down the right-field line and hummed the throw home, catching our second baseman before he could cross the plate. It was really a thrill seeing this man throw from the outfield.

Roy Campanella was catching then for the Caguas team. He was a strong, stocky young man with sure hands.

Guayama, my team, finished the season one game behind Ponce, a team managed by one of the greatest Negro old-time stars, George Scales.

Gibson didn't hit .500 that year, but he did lead the league, batting .473, and still hit more home runs than anybody else that season.

I led the league in triples and RBIs, but my blistering .360 batting average got lost in the shadow of Gibson's bat.

The league promoted an all-star game between the Puerto Ricans and the Americans; Josh and I were selected to catch for the Americans.

The Puerto Rican team featured the powerful slugging of Coimbre, Perucho Cepeda, and Luis Olmo. But I just couldn't get over how great Josh was in Puerto Rico. Man, he was something else!

6
TWO BALL PLAYERS
WORTH EIGHTY
THOUSAND WORKERS

The time had come to make up my mind about the next season, and I decided I wanted to play in Mexico City. I wrote George Pasquel, who held the highest position of authority in the league, and—knowing his word was law—asked to be traded to Mexico City. I received his reply within a few weeks; my request was approved.

All the Americans sailed for home in 1942 on the same ship, departing from San Juan, Puerto Rico, and arriving in New York after four days at sea. During the voyage, Roy Campanella and Monte Irvin conferred with me about the prospects of playing ball in Mexico. In those days, most players wanted to go to Mexico because of advantages such as a lack of many off-schedule games and the fact that all expenses were paid.

I knew there were two positions open in the Mexican League. One was with my old team, Monterrey, and the other opening was because of Josh Gibson's not playing in Mexico that season. I detailed what was happening and promised to recommend them to the clubs.

After arriving in New York, most of the players went uptown to Harlem for a day, but I headed straight for Grand Central Station.

When I got home I found that everything was indeed not the same. We had drifted apart, and I blamed myself for having been away so much and so long.

Hello–good-bye—I stayed for only a week, then took off again for Mexico.

Monte Irvin joined the Veracruz team a few days after I arrived in Mexico City. We both were staying at one of the big hotels, but after a couple of weeks we decided to get an apartment together. A little later on we read in the newspaper that Campanella had joined the Monterrey team.

The day before the first game, Campanella came to our apartment and cooked a big pot of spaghetti. The three of us really had a lot of fun playing chef on different parts of the dinner.

I wore Campy's team out, and in the last game of the series, after I had hit my third home run, he said to me, "Quincy, don't expect me to cook any more spaghetti when I come to Mexico City. It must have given you extra power!"

With hopes of improving our family relationship, Dorothy and the children joined me in Mexico. Monte's wife also came to be with him.

Monte was trying to fill Josh's shoes. Gibson had played only three-quarters of the season the year before, but had achieved a record thirty-three home runs. Monte did not do much hitting the first three weeks, and one day, as I was leaving the clubhouse on my way to the playing field, George Pasquel, owner of the Veracruz team, stopped me to ask a few questions about Monte.

"Hey, Troupe, what's the matter with this Irvin? No bat, no nothing. You told me he was a good player. What's the matter?" he asked me in Spanish.

"Well, the season is still young. I think he will come around okay. Give him a little time and he'll do a good job for you," I told him.

"I'll take your word for it, Troupe. Let's see if things will change for the better."

Monte started showing his ability that same day, hitting a home run and two singles. He ended the season by winning the batting championship; he hit around the .390 mark and knocked in twenty-two home runs.

As for me, I had my best year yet in Mexico, hitting a solid .360 and fifteen home runs. In 1942 I was selected to catch in the big all-star game for the south in Mexico City. The south that year was made up of the Mexico City Reds, Veracruz, and Pueblo. The north's players were from Monterrey, Tampico, and Torreon.

Unfortunately, just one week before the game, my hand was lacerated between my index and middle fingers. It put me out of action for three weeks, and I missed the all-star contest. Campanella replaced me and played a bang-up game. I believe he got three hits—one a home run. Our team won by a big margin.

One day Bill Wright came over and stood by me at the batting cage. "There's a scout here from the Dodgers. He wants to talk to you, Theolic, Silvio, and me. We're to see him after the game."

Looking toward the stands, I spotted a stranger and asked, "Is that the guy back there?"

"Yes," Bill said. "His name is Greenwade."

If I did not show much enthusiasm it was because I had heard so much talk in the past about my playing in the majors and not a thing had happened. Talk about any black man playing in the major leagues was just not something to get excited about.

As things turned out, I was right. The guy was not at his hotel where he had said he wanted to meet us. It was just another false alarm.

Returning to St. Louis at the close of the season, I, like everyone else, got caught up in the war.

I sold my car because it was too difficult to get gas stamps. I tried to enlist, but I was turned down because of my dependents. So I went to work in a defense plant, hoping my new way of life would be good for me and my family.

TWO BALL PLAYERS WORTH EIGHTY THOUSAND WORKERS

Then spring 1943 came and brought with it a letter from George Pasquel, asking me to play in Mexico. Dorothy and I talked about it, and I wrote to Pasquel and told him I could not leave St. Louis or play in Mexico that season. My job classification at the defense plant kept me from leaving the country.

Pasquel got in touch with my draft board and the Curtis Wright Aircraft Company, where I was employed as an inspector. He worked things out, and I was free to leave. I was eager to go, and yet forlorn. Dorothy, as always, told me good-bye.

In '43, Chile Gomez, an ex–major leaguer who had played second base for the Phillies, was traded from Pueblo to the Veracruz team in Mexico City. Pueblo in turn brought up Roberto Avila from Veracruz. He was of medium build, around 150 pounds, and stood five-nine.

The first time I saw him in action was one Sunday when we played Pueblo in a double-header. In those two games he showed me he had something the ordinary player just does not have.

He was not a good hitter at this point, but he stood up there at the plate with confidence, taking a good level cut at the ball.

When I came up to bat I hit a line shot into the outfield. Old-timers had told me to always hustle to first base, and I made that advice a part of my playing style. On a fumble you can also reach second if you have hustled to first.

Well, I was really digging in, figuring I would make my turn around first, and if the outfielder did anything slow, or fumbled the ball, I would go on to second. I glanced in the direction in which I had hit the ball without breaking stride, and as I was about three-quarters of the way from first and home, I saw Roberto go over, backhand the ball, stop, and, almost at the same time, make a long, sidearm throw to first. Despite how hard I had turned it on, the throw beat me by one step.

"Well," I thought to myself, "this youngster is green, playing out of position. He just made that catch by luck."

The next time I came to bat, the same pitcher was working. He had no reason to play me any differently than last time, and I hit one between him and the first baseman. The first baseman almost made an attempt to field the ball, but he stopped short and covered first. To my surprise this young green kid came up with the ball and threw me out by a couple of steps. He was just a raw rookie without experience, yet he made plays that day that would be trouble for anyone other than top pros.

After the game, I left the hotel to have dinner. I ran into Avila at a corner and stopped to commend him on his great play. My Spanish was pretty good by now.

"How are you? Aren't you Roberto Avila?" I asked him.

"Yes," he replied.

"You looked really great out there today."

"Thank you very much."

His manner and his smile indicated he was pleased I had stopped to talk to him in his native tongue. At that time I was a leading player in the Mexican League, and he was impressed with my record, as young players always are when they meet experienced men. "You have what it takes to go as high in baseball as you want," I found myself telling him. "When someone tells you something, just listen. Don't get the big head, and I think you'll make it." It brought back memories of Satch, and Mule, and the old St. Louis Stars, and the things they had told me. My, how time does fly.

"Thanks again. I'll remember what you told me," Avila said.

❖ ❖ ❖

Our next series was back in Mexico City against Monterrey. In a game with Lazaro Salazar pitching for Monterrey, I struck out my first time at bat, hitting right-handed, and the second time at bat I hit a weak ground ball for an easy out. The third time up I decided to bat on my left side against the left-handed pitcher, and again Salazar got me out.

The next time I came to bat we had one man on base. The manager, Carmona, who was coaching on the third-base line, called to me down the line halfway between third and home: "Quincy, I want you to bat on your right side. I don't care if you strike out, or what happens. Bat right-handed, will you?"

It really helped having the manager back me like that.

Returning to home plate, I had the feeling that at least everything was okay, regardless of what happened, so I batted right-handed.

Salazar was a very smart man in baseball, one who had been a manager himself for several years. I figured he was smart enough to know that with left field only 310 feet out, a curve was not the best pitch to throw at this stage of the game. So I was looking for a fast ball, and when it came I swung, hitting a line drive to center field. I was running hard, rounding first base, when I heard my first-base coach shout, "Take it easy, the ball is over the fence!" This was quite a surprise to me, even knowing the ball travels farther in Mexico City because of the high altitude.

We finally won that game in the ninth inning on a home run by Salvatierra.

That same season, my wife filed for a separation, charging I was away from home too much. I finally signed the papers, and she got a divorce and custody of our two boys. My rising baseball career had taken its toll on my domestic life.

My teammate Bill Wright, who was from Los Angeles, formed a team with me to play winter ball in California. Our team consisted of Ray Dandridge, Terris "Speed" McDuffie, Willard Brown, and other well-known sepia stars.

The first game we played was in San Diego against Buck "Bobo" Newsome's All Stars.

I was sitting on the edge of the dugout, lacing up my shoes, when someone tapped my shoulder. "Archie Moore! How are you doing, man?" I jumped up and grabbed his hand.

"Hi, Quincy, how's everything?"

"I'm fine, Archie. Say, I heard you're living here now?"

"Right. I think I'll make this my home. I really like it out here. You still whaling on that ball?"

"Well, I had a pretty good season this year in Mexico. I've been playing there since 1939."

"I know," Archie confided, "I've been keeping up with you. Quincy, come on over to the stands, I'd like you to meet some of my friends."

Archie introduced me to his friends, and they all wished me well in the game. It's always nice to know you have people out in the stands pulling for you.

Buck Newsome had developed a pitch that was called "the blooper ball." The first time I came to bat, he threw it to me and I hit the ball off the top of the left-field fence for two bases. The next time I came to bat, people started yelling at Newsome to throw me that pitch again. Newsome didn't want to show the people he was afraid to throw his blooper to me; he let his emotions get the upper hand on his judgment.

We were playing in a stadium built for football. Left field was short, but right field was a good six hundred feet away. Newsome started out all right with a fast ball, but it was high. A big fat man behind Buck's dugout yelled, "Hey, Buck, you better not throw Troupe that blooper ball again!"

Newsome went back to his blooper, and it came in high too. A lot of other fans started acting like the fat man.

Newsome reared back and threw. I connected on that ball, hitting it deep into right field. The outfielder knew the ball was far over his head, and he turned around and started running. The ball fell ten yards beyond him and rolled to the fence. Before he could retrieve it I had rounded the bases for an inside-the-park home run.

After the game, I met Archie and we talked about old times. I had been keeping up with him and complimented him on his outstanding boxing record.

Archie told me he figured I would leave boxing and return to baseball, because I did not have a fighter's heart. "Quincy, I don't think you could ever be a fighter. You're just too nice. You're not the mean type. You've got to have a certain meanness in your disposition to make it as a fighter, and I don't think you have it. Now don't get me wrong. You have the punch. You move faster than the average heavyweight, and you've got a real sharp left jab. But you are not mean."

His remarks were very interesting. They gave me insight into my lack of desire to become a prizefighter.

The next day the newspaper stated that the home run I hit off of Buck Newsome was a five-hundred-foot record-breaker. I had moved into winter ball in California with a bang.

After the season closed I went to work in the engineering department of one of the aircraft plants. I played basketball on the plant team.

My defense-plant work involved inspection on the assembly line, and I really liked it, but when spring arrived that old baseball fever hit me again. I got a leave of absence from my job and returned to St. Louis.

There was still a war going on, and it was time to check with the draft board again. The team in Mexico City wanted me back, so I tried to get a permit to go to Mexico, but the draft board turned me down flat. Once again, I wrote George Pasquel in Mexico City.

While I was mulling things over about returning to California and my job, I was contacted by the Mexican consul at my home. The representative from Mexico told me that they had loaned the United States eighty thousand workers to fill the manpower shortage caused by the war, and that all they asked in return were two ball players—Quincy Troupe and Theolic Smith!

George Pasquel was a powerful man. It still staggers my mind how he was able to bring about this astounding exchange.

After a couple of visits to the Mexican consul office, Theolic Smith and I were given permission to go to Mexico, and eighty thousand Mexican workers crossed the American border to beef up the American war effort.

◆ ◆ ◆

In 1944, after playing a few months in Mexico, I received a letter from the Cleveland Buckeyes. The owner had made me an offer to become player-manager. I played a few postseason games with the Buckeyes, surveying the team without the players being aware of my intentions.

It soon became obvious to me that the team needed a shortstop and a second catcher.

In Mexico that year I had noticed Avelino Canizares, a shortstop from Cuba.

Sam Jethroe and I went to Puerto Rico that year to play with the San Juan team. I tried to get a permit to go to Cuba to sign Canizares, but the owner of my team would not give me permission. He also talked to some of the people at the airport and made it impossible for me to get a reservation. Since reservations during the war were given on a priority scale, I needed help; I got it from a friend on another team, who sent me to the owner. The man arranged a permit and reservation for me, and I was off to Cuba.

There I was to play with the Marianao team, but I was overweight when I arrived. I had to lose a few pounds fast. I started playing my usual game by the second week, but by then the newspaper had already started riding me, charging that I could not hit and that the only way I could get on base was by the pitcher walking me.

Most of the players knew better than that, having faced me in Mexico, and the pitchers tried to keep from giving me anything good to hit. That was the real reason I received so many bases-on-balls.

But maybe the sportswriters and my overweight condition convinced the pitchers I really couldn't hit, because finally they began to pitch to me, and I started peppering the ball again. The sportswriters soon retracted their statements.

I ended the season hitting .317, with a lot of new fans cheering for Troupe. Avelino Canizares and a catcher signed the contracts I offered them, and I brought them back with me to the States.

◆ ◆ ◆

When I went into spring training my first year as manager, I stressed one thing: fundamentals. I also came right out and predicted that my team would be the new champions in the Negro Baseball League.

7

THE CLEVELAND BUCKEYES VS. THE HOMESTEAD GRAYS

The 1945 season started with the Cleveland Buckeyes getting out front on top of the standings.

We played the Kansas City Monarchs in Belleville, Illinois, when they were carrying a shortstop by the name of Jackie Robinson.

Jackie was a real fireball. He loved to win. We won the game in Belleville, and afterward, when both teams were dressing in the locker room, Jackie got into it with my outfielders, Sam Jethroe and Buddy Armour. He really had a sharp tongue, and I wondered who this young cat was to be raising all that sand.

Later that season I played against him again in Cleveland, and he overpowered my pitcher's curve with a line drive into the left-field stands. I knew then he had the makings of a top pro. When a young player breaks into pro ball hitting the curve with authority, you can expect to see him develop into an excellent hitter.

Although he had the makings of a real good player, I think it came as a surprise when word got out that the Brooklyn Dodgers had signed him to a contract. It was hard to imagine any black player cracking the major leagues, and with Jackie's temper being the way it was, it didn't seem likely that a major-league team would be willing to take a chance with him. The golden dream, the impossible golden dream of sepia players roaming the ball fields of the major leagues, was now crystallizing into reality at last.

Jim "Candy" Taylor was managing the Chicago American Giants in '45. His reputation was known to me before I ever entered pro baseball, and he was one of the great Negro managers. He gave me a few tips I'll never forget. I think they are some of the most important things you need to know when managing a baseball club.

"Try to understand your men," he told me. "Know their abilities, and know when to change pitchers."

There was one more thing I picked up from Candy: I kept my personal business to myself. I believe this is vital for the morale of the team.

The rest of the league never could get by us that season, and when the big East-West game rolled around, I was voted in by the fans to catch for the West.

The game was played in Chicago, as usual, before a crowd of forty-five thousand fans.

Playing in the East-West game was always a thrill, but there was something even more challenging that year. I was really bearing down, concentrating on the Cleveland Buckeyes and living up to my prediction, when the thrill of thrills materialized: we won the Western Negro League championship during my first year of managing the team. That put us right square in front of another big bad mountain. We had a play-off series ahead of us with the Homestead Grays.

And who did the Homestead Grays have on their team? Just Josh Gibson, Sam Bankhead, Buck Leonard, Ray Brown, Jerry Benjamin, Howard Easterling, Cool Papa Bell, Roy Welmaker, and a few other guys.

I had a very young team, and naturally most of them looked up to the Grays. But, even though it may not have been generally recognized, I knew how really good my own team was. The Cleveland Buckeyes were not a fluke. We had Avelino Canizares at shortstop, playing just as much ball as Robinson. Canizares could judge hitters with unbelievable accuracy, and he held the infield together by keeping everyone alerted to the abilities of each hitter.

I had drilled our pitchers on how to work with me in getting the batter to go for the bad pitch. Believe me, we dragged every trick out of the trunk and added a few new ones. My guys knew how to get their pitches somewhere over that plate when they had to.

We weren't known as a power outfit, although we had players besides myself who could park one on you quick, but what we were doing that caught everyone by surprise and got us by them was bringing back the old brand of ball playing made famous in Rube Foster's heyday. Back then, guys like Jelly Gardner and Jimmy Lyons could drive you crazy by choking up on the bat, getting a piece of that ball, laying down a bunt, executing the hit-and-run, hitting behind the runner, and running wild stealing on the base paths. It was true the Homestead Grays could bomb you out of the park, but my team was very fast. We could run the tongue out of anybody's head.

Well, no one thought we had much of a chance, and when game time arrived the Grays breezed in full of confidence. We were all using the same locker room, and they rode the backs of my team like we were their favorite horse. Josh called us a string of bad names, as colorful as they were long, describing how they were going to pour it on us all over the park. All the way from here to Philadelphia, where we would be playing our fourth game, they were going to grind us up into hamburger meat, Gibson promised.

My guys didn't have too much to say. As a matter of fact, they didn't say anything. They just sat there soaking it all in.

Finally, I did have something to say to my team. Usually in clubhouse meetings, I had a lot to say before the game about the opposing team, but in this series I knew the problem was to try to get through to my players and ease the tension, so I just told them to go out there and play this one like it was just another game.

And, man, did they play! The more the Grays heckled us during the game, the harder my team hustled.

After the first game, which we managed to win, the Grays were still heckling. My team didn't say a word.

Game number two came, and we won that one, too. Believe me, by now, the Grays were no longer joking.

Well, as a matter of fact, we whipped the Grays four straight games. The last two were shutouts, and that really shut them up. They couldn't help themselves. They were in deep shock. They just couldn't believe it. And I'll admit, it was hard for some of our guys to believe it, too, but there was no disputing the fact that the Cleveland Buckeyes were the newly crowned champs of the Negro Baseball League. I was really proud of our team, and there was something else buoying me up—I wound up the leading hitter in the series.

Now Josh Gibson was not the type of guy to stay quiet too long, and after the series most of the players went to New Orleans for the North-South game, which was an annual event much like the East-West contest in Chicago.

In Houston, Texas, Josh put on a hitting exhibition before the game, hitting shot after shot out of the park in every direction while the crowd looked on in amazement.

After he'd finished one of the fellows asked, "How many bats do you break in a season?"

Josh just looked at the guy and grinned. "Man, I don't break bats," he said. "I just wear them out."

8
TOURING SOUTH AMERICA WITH JACKIE ROBINSON

After the season was over in 1945, Blanco Chitaiqe, a Venezuelan consul official, got in touch with me about playing on a team he had put together to tour Venezuela for two months. The name of the team was the American All Stars, and old-timer Felton Snow was to be its manager. Besides Jackie Robinson and myself, the team was made up of Buck Leonard, Roy Campanella, Sam Jethroe, Marvin Barker, Bill Anderson, George Jefferson, Parnel Woods, Roy Welmaker, Eugene Benson, and Verdell Mathis.

I was interviewed by Ray Gillespie of the St. Louis Star Times just before leaving town.

Ray wanted to know if there were any other sepia players I knew besides Jackie Robinson that were good enough to make the majors. Well, I could have told him he was talking to an excellent major-league prospect himself.

I did tell him about Don Newcombe and Monte Irvin, as well as Sam Jethroe, our Cleveland Buckeyes center fielder who made the big play all season long, wore out opposing pitchers, and forced our challengers to respect his speed on the base paths.

My wife, Dorothy, and I officially separated in 1945. All the traveling had finally worn her out with me being gone all the time. We still loved each other, but we had just grown apart. I was sad to leave her and my two sons, but she thought it was for the best. But man, it sure did hurt me.

The American All Stars assembled in New York, and we had to get passports, shots, and doctors' certificates before they let us fly over to Caracas, Venezuela.

Jackie Robinson's temper was a real problem for his friends. Due to his inability to cool it, we were worried about him making the grade. I remember one day when Felton Snow tried to talk to Jackie about the right way to handle a certain play at shortstop, and Jackie really talked back to him bad. After he got through talking he wouldn't listen to one word Felton had to say.

But things weren't always tense. We had a lot of good times, too. Campy and I were with Jackie when he bought the engagement ring in Caracas for

Rachel, who later became his wife, and of course Jackie did come through and do a real good job, making it big in the big leagues in spite of his temper.

We had a lot of fun on the flight we took to Maracaibo. All our guys got to singing Christmas carols and were joined by Beatrice Werner, a pretty stewardess and a loyal fan. The stewardesses were the center of attraction, as they perched on the sides of the seats, singing along with us.

After a while the other passengers joined in.

It was a beautiful flight. I experienced a feeling then I had come to know in many strange places—a sense of inner warmth from the glow in faces of friendly people who reached out and let you know you were wanted and among the best of friends.

The first time I had known this feeling was when Señor Ferrara met Eugene Smith and me in Nueva Laredo, Mexico. He really made us feel welcome, and that was a gracious thing to do for strangers.

As the plane came over Maracaibo, the flight became rough, but we landed okay.

We were met at the airport by several city officials, and they had special cars waiting to take us to the best hotel. Best or not, the mosquitoes almost ate us alive that night.

Christmas Day, my birthday, was really hot. We Americans had never played ball in such heat before. It was so bad that Campanella and I traded off playing the outfield and catching during each half of the game. We played several games in Maracaibo, then returned the first of the year to Caracas.

The first months of '46 found the big leagues on a lot of players' minds.

Campanella was just living to get a chance with the Dodgers. It was all he thought and talked about. When the letter from the Dodgers organization finally arrived, he was the happiest person in the hotel, and it was no problem at all for us to imagine how he felt.

They wanted him to report early for spring training, and the days couldn't go by fast enough for Campy to get away.

During the time he was waiting we often talked about catching. I filled him in on a lot of tricks I had picked up from guys who helped me. "Roy," I said, "a lot of people think a good catcher is just a guy who receives the ball well and has a good arm, but you and I know that ain't even scratching the surface. Man, a good fifteen years ago an old-timer named Young told me a few things that are still helping today. You see, there are several kinds of hitters, and the catcher is the man who has to detect each type and know what to do. A man has to have the instinct for this to be a good catcher."

"Quincy, what kinds of hitters are there?" Roy wanted to know.

"Well, I would say there are three—the guy that hits with his foot in the bucket, the guy who stands up there flat-footed, and the lunger."

"Yeah, I hear you," Roy said.

"Yeah, but each of these types can have a different kind of swing, or have the same kind of swing with a different kind of stance."

"Now, wait a minute, Quincy, I'm not with you now."

"A chop swinger, we usually say, is a high-ball hitter."

"Yeah, that's right," Roy agreed.

"Uh-huh, but the movement of his body can either be bucket, flat-footed, or lunging."

"Aw, yeah. Look, Quincy, take each type, one by one, and explain it to me," Roy said.

"Okay. And I'll try to tell you how I'd pitch to each type. For instance, for a chop swinger, I'd pitch just the opposite to the way I would to an up swinger."

"What about a man who swings level at the ball?"

"Well, usually, he's a real good hitter. If he knows the strike zone, he's pretty hard to get out. Now, let's come back to his position at the plate. If he lunges, hits flat-footed, or pulls, I'd pitch according to that. A man who lunges, I'd pitch in on. If a man pulls, I'd pitch away, and if he's flat-footed, I'd either pitch up, or down. When you have played against him long enough, you'll know which is best."

"You know, Quincy, that's good technique. Mackey has talked to me about some things too."

"Roy, I know these tips will do you a lot of good with the Dodgers. The hitters in the majors know the strike zone, so you've got to make every pitch count. I've played long enough to know that there are few players who can hit the ball well anywhere in the strike zone. To find the weak spot of any hitter, watch for his type and play him according to that."

"Quincy, what about the different pitches, like the curve, fast ball, and change-up?"

"Usually you apply the same thing I've just explained. You curve away, or low inside. On the fast ball, you go away or inside. But on the change-up, you have to pick the men you throw it to. Most times you don't throw a flat-footed hitter a change-up, and sometimes that goes with other types as well."

I paused, knowing I had been doing a lot of talking.

"Go on," Roy urged.

"Well, you'll find in the long run, percentage is the best policy. Always have your pitcher pitch the easiest and safest way to get a batter out. I remember one time in Cuba I was playing with Marianao. The manager had talked to the pitcher and me in the clubhouse about every player on the opposing team's lineup. He cautioned us not to let one particular hitter he named hit the fast ball in the pinch. Well, in the game, we were leading in the late innings by one run. The first man grounded out, and the next two men got on, and here was that man we had talked about in the clubhouse coming up to take his cut. The first pitch was a curve strike. The next curve he fouled off for strike two. I signaled for a bad fast ball, and the pitcher threw one high inside. I then called for another curve ball, but this guy stayed alive up there, fouling it off. We tried faking him out with another bad fast ball, but he let it go by, and the count was now two and two. Well now, I decided, was a good time to really get tricky, and I used the old routine of indirectly talking to my pitcher loud enough for this guy to hear what the next pitch would be."

"Yeah," Roy nodded, understanding what I meant.

"So I called for the curve and signaled for a fast ball to catch a piece of the plate."

"Yeah," Roy said.

"Uh huh. And the last time I saw that ball a spectator was trying to catch it in the stands."

"Yeah," Roy said. "He really unloaded on you, eh?"

"Yeah, and that's the point. Always make a batter hit the pitch that's best to get him out with. Don't get carried away getting fancy with tricks. Sometimes you will get by trying to fool the hitter, but many times you will get stung. All hitters have become accustomed to a particular way of hitting through the years."

"Yeah, I see what you mean."

"Now, the most important thing, other than knowing the hitter, is to understand the temperament of the pitcher. You must go out and talk to him every so often. You'll find sometimes you'll have to get rough and bawl him out. Then, there's the other type of pitcher you must encourage, using almost exactly the opposite approach. Any catcher who can master this will definitely go places if he has the physical qualifications."

Marvin Williams came down from his room, joining us in the lobby. "Let's go, you dummies. Play the game on the field. We'll be late for the first movie," he said.

"Honestly, Marvin, aren't you ever serious about anything?" Roy asked.

"Serious? Hell, no. That kind of stuff will give you ulcers," Marvin said.

We only lost two games during the whole tour.

◆ ◆ ◆

After the American All Star tour I signed with the Venezuelan League. Two teams were interested in me, and I finally decided to play with the Magallanes Club.

Alexander Carrasquel was pitching with this team. He was a pitcher in the majors and had been with several clubs. Luis Aparicio was at shortstop, a real demon with the glove. He was past thirty at this time, and not too much of a hitter, but he was a full-fledged major leaguer in every other respect. My agreement with the club called for my leaving Venezuela early enough to make spring training in the U.S.A.

Cool Papa Bell again helped Quincy's baseball career by mentioning him to the owner of the Monterrey, Mexico, Carta Blanca team. This 1939 photo shows Quincy (back row, center) during his first year with the team. Many African American players opted for Mexico, where they could be taken more seriously as players and managers. Courtesy Quincy Troupe, Jr.

Quincy Troupe, Jr., was born in the United States during Quincy, Sr.'s, first year in Mexico, 1939. His mother-in-law phoned him with the news. Courtesy Quincy Troupe, Jr.

A postcard showing Quincy at bat for Carta Blanca, 1940. Courtesy Quincy Troupe, Jr.

Monte Irvin and Quincy Troupe, off the field in Monterrey,
Mexico, 1940. Courtesy Quincy Troupe, Jr.

A portrait taken during Quincy's last season playing for Carta Blanca, 1941.
Courtesy Quincy Troupe, Jr.

In 1942 Quincy left Carta Blanca to play for the Mexico City Reds. This photo captures him tagging out a player at home plate while playing for the Reds in 1943. Courtesy Quincy Troupe, Jr.

Quincy's second son, Timothy, was also born while Troupe was away playing in Mexico. In 1943 the growing Troupe family traveled to Mexico to visit the ball player, producing this family portrait. Courtesy Quincy Troupe, Jr.

Back in the States in 1945, Quincy accepted a position as player-manager with the Cleveland Buckeyes. Not only did the team win the Western Negro League championship that year, but they also swept the great Homestead Grays in a four-game play-off series. Here J. Cowan (left) and A. Carnzaries (right) relax with Quincy after winning the final game 5-0. Courtesy Quincy Troupe, Jr.

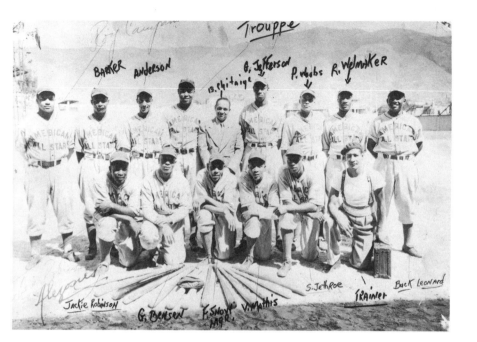

Also in 1945, Blanco Chataiqe, a Venezuelan consulate official, convinced Quincy to play on the American All Stars team. The team, which included Roy Campanella, Buck Leonard, and Jackie Robinson, barnstormed all over Venezuela. Back row, left to right: Roy Campanella, Baltimore Elites; Marvin Barker, New York Black Yankees; B. Anderson, New York Black Yankees; Quincy Troupe, Cleveland Buckeyes; Blanco Chataiqe; George Jefferson, Cleveland Buckeyes; Parnel Woods, Cleveland Buckeyes; Roy Welmaker, Homestead Grays; Buck Leonard, Homestead Grays. Front row, left to right: Jackie Robinson, Kansas City Monarchs; Eugene Benson, Philadelphia Stars; Felton Snow, Baltimore Elites; Verdell Mathis, Memphis Red Sox; Sam Jethroe, Cleveland Buckeyes. Courtesy Quincy Troupe, Jr.

An argument at home plate, the Cleveland Buckeyes vs. the Memphis Red Sox, 1946. From left to right: Chet Brewer, George Minor, Willie Grace, Archie Ware (Cleveland Buckeyes); Jelly Taylor (no. 35) and Casey Jones (Memphis Red Sox). The umpire, hidden by Taylor, is Spoon Carter. Courtesy Quincy Troupe, Jr.

A more relaxed moment, possibly after the same Buckeyes–Red Sox game. Cleveland Buckeye players Frank Caldwell and Elijah Chism (left) with Chet Brewer and Vibert Clark (right) tease Buddy Armour (center) about his game-saving catch. Courtesy Quincy Troupe, Jr.

9
PLAYERS I DEVELOPED IN THE U.S.A.

1946 was the year many players from organized baseball were going to Mexico. Ted Williams and Joe DiMaggio were given offers to play down below the border. Many ball players from Latin countries also went to Mexico. While I was playing in Venezuela, I contracted two players, Vibert Clarke and Leon Kellman, both from Panama. It was also the year I added a p to my last name and became Trouppe (pronounced "Troo-pay") instead of Troupe. That's what they called me in Mexico, and I just grew to like the sound of it.

When I returned to the States, I found Mexico had gotten to my team, too. The Buckeyes' shortstop had gone there to play ball. We had several other key positions missing, too, and I had to start building all over again.

We went to St. Louis for an exhibition game, and John Brisko, a newspaper photographer friend of mine, came to the hotel to talk about a young shortstop he believed I ought to meet.

"What's his name?"

"Al Smith. I think he would make a good boy for your team."

"Well, John, you know me. Bring him by about an hour before we leave for the park. I'd like to talk to him."

Within half an hour Brisko came through the lobby door with the young man. We talked until it was time to go to the park.

Al Smith impressed me immediately. He showed plenty of confidence, and I took him along with the team. His hitting was very good from the start. I played him at shortstop for the rest of the season.

We played the Homestead Grays in an exhibition game in Buffalo, New York, and during the game I kidded Josh Gibson after he had swung and missed. "Hey, man! Why you want to be so mean? If you had connected on that one, those people on the porch over there behind center field would have had to scramble to get out of the way!"

Josh did not have a comeback for my remarks, and that was unusual for him. I learned later he was having trouble with his legs. But, the next time at bat, he hit a drive over the center field fence, and those folks across the way did have to move to keep from getting hit by the ball.

That very next year, 1947, Josh Gibson died. The golden dream, for him, would always remain unfulfilled.

◆ ◆ ◆

The Kansas City Monarchs got by us and won the championship. They entered the play-offs against the Newark Eagles, who had Monte Irvin, Johnny Davis, Lennie Pearson, and Bizz Mackey.

After the play-offs, Satchel Paige formed an all-star team to play against Bob Feller's All Stars.

I would be the catcher for Satchel's team.

Two planes were chartered, and we flew to our opening in Pittsburgh, with Satchel and Feller working three innings each.

Barney Brown finished for us, and Lemon finished for Feller.

Sugar Ray Robinson, who was really in his prime then, sat in our dugout during the game. His picture was taken with Satchel and Feller.

I came to bat in the third, hitting left-handed against Feller, a right-handed pitcher, and hit a line drive over the third baseman's head and down the left-field line for two bases. Just as I reached second, Phil Rizutto took the relay from left field and turned toward me before tossing the ball to Feller. "Boy, you hit 'em the way he pitches, eh?" he said.

I couldn't help but smile. The game ended 3-1 in our favor.

We played our next game before twenty-seven thousand fans at Yankee Stadium in New York. In that game, Jeff Heath robbed me of a homer by spearing a ball I had hammered off of Chandler just before it dipped into the right-field stands.

Nick Stanley finished the game for us in good form. Nick could do everything to the ball. He threw a spitball curve, fast-ball sinker, screwball, and shine ball—that scuffed-up baseball Roosevelt Davis was so mean with. We hung a goose egg on them in that game, 4-0.

Feller's boys had never hit against this type of pitching before, especially the spitball.

Nick really made them look bad, and in front of all those fans. They were so upset over Nick's pitching they would not play another game until we released him from the team. That made me wonder about the younger generation of hitters. There were many pitchers like Nick, twenty-five years before he threw his first ball.

We moved across the river to Newark, New Jersey. I got two home runs and a single in that game, which we won easily.

Feller's team came back strong, winning in Youngstown, Cleveland, and Chicago. We played from New York throughout the west, ending our tour in Kansas City, Missouri.

In the Kansas City game, Chandler was pitching for Feller and Barney Brown for Satch.

Feller's team was leading us 2-1 going into the ninth. In the last inning, our first man up grounded to short, and the next batter received a base-on-balls.

This brought up Johnny Davis, who had been murdering the ball all through the tour. Johnny didn't let us down. With the count at one and one,

Chandler's curve hung on the inside of the plate, and Davis drove it far over the left-field fence, winning the game for us, 3-2.

I returned to Venezuela and had another good season. Sam Neham was my battery mate, and our team finished in second place. The next season, Sam got his chance with the Phillies.

◆ ◆ ◆

Spring training, 1947. The Buckeyes were in Orlando, Florida, playing an exhibition game against a local team that had a big boy pitching for them by the name of Sam Jones. He struck out ten Buckeyes that day, and after the game we all had dinner together. I spoke to Jones about playing for the Buckeyes. At that time he was still in the service, but he promised to contact me when he got out that summer.

After spring training we always played a few games on our way home, and I always reminded my boys to try not to get into any kind of hassle with white southerners. I routed our schedule so that we would be eating at black cafés, where we could use rest room facilities without any trouble. I really took pains to work it out like that, because I must say I had a team of strong, healthy young men who didn't believe in taking crap off of anybody.

Our second day on the road we had to stop in a small town in Arkansas to get gas, and the boys got off the bus to take a stretch. We had been riding a long time.

We had been there a half-hour when some of the guys went over to the store to buy something.

Just before everybody returned to the bus, a couple of white guys came over, walking fast like the road belonged to them. We hadn't gotten their permission to pass.

I was just about to board the bus when one of my boys said, "Hey, Skip, those two guys coming up here said some pretty nasty things a few minutes ago in that store. I know what you said, and we ignored what they had to say once, but we damn sure ain't going to take it again."

The white guys came over and looked at the Cleveland Buckeyes sign painted on the side of our bus.

"Might have known you coons is from the north," the tall one said.

"Yeah, niggers from the north don't know how to act in Arkansas," his big, red-faced companion said.

"I guess we gonna have to show these shines—"

That was as far as they got. The two players they had been riding in the store lit into them, planting knuckle sandwiches all over their heads. When it was all over, two southern white men were lying stretched-out cold on the hard, sun-baked ground of Arkansas.

"Okay, you guys, let's saddle up and get out of here," I said.

We did, too, putting fifty miles between us before slowing down to normal speed when I noticed a highway patrolman parked in a gasoline station in a small town.

When we were about a block and a half away the patrolman pulled out behind the bus. He came on pretty fast, and by the time we were at the edge of town, he had put his siren on and pulled us over.

With all the commotion going on everyone aboard was now wide awake.

I turned around in my seat and said, "Don't nobody say a word. I'll do all the talking."

The patrolman pulled up and parked in back of the bus. He got out slowly and proceeded to walk up to our bus, where he checked the license plates, then went around to the side and looked at the Cleveland Buckeyes sign.

After that he puffed all up like a cobra and headed toward the front door of the bus.

The bus driver opened the door, and the officer stepped inside. He looked down one side, and up the other, then back to me and the bus driver. "Who is in charge of this outfit?"

"I am officer. Is there anything wrong with the bus?"

He looked straight at me. "You know damn well what I'm here for, and I want to know right now which one of you uppity niggers did it."

I looked him straight in the eye. "Officer, I'm in charge of this team. We travel from Texas to Canada, and all over the United States. Sometimes we don't even see a bed in three or four days, but we never miss playing a ball game, unless we get rained out. Now, me and the team have been catching up on some long overdue sleep. I know the guys are just as worn out and tired and sleepy as I am. I doubt if anybody has been awake long enough to know what is going on."

"Well, I got a report that a gang of coons on this bus jumped on some white men. Now niggers all look alike to me, so I guess I ain't going to be able to lock nobody up, but I am going to tell you one thing, and none of you better not ever forget it. A nigger just don't hit a white man in Arkansas. We still know how to skin a darky's ass clean as a whistle, by gawd, and you better keep that on your mind every second you're traveling through the south."

He stepped down off the bus, returned to his car, stopped, looked back at us for a minute, then got in, started up, and gunned his motor as he passed our bus, still parked on the side of the road.

"That son-of-a-bitch sure do speak bad behind a pistol and a badge," Parnel Woods said.

"If you run into a white man in any part of the world other than places like South Africa and the southern United States, you'll find him acting like a human being. He only treats you the way that cop was acting when he feels he can get away with it," I said. "Okay, Charles, let's get the show back on the road. We still have a game to play in Little Rock tonight."

◆ ◆ ◆

Chippy Britt and Parnel Woods were pounding their fists in the palms of their hands and grinning like crazy when we pulled into the parking lot at the Traveler's Stadium in Little Rock.

About two months later we were in Cleveland, making preparations for a trip to Chicago, when I received a telegram from Sam Jones. He was ready to join the ball club. I had a talk with the business manager, Wilbur Hayes. "Wilbur, I think the best thing for you to do is to take a plane down there and bring the boy back. You never can tell what might happen if we send him the money. He could change his mind, you know."

Hayes went over to the dresser drawer and took some money from it. "Well, Quincy, you better take this money for expenses for the tour. I'll try to be back here when you return home."

"Okay, Wilbur, and I hope you have a lot of luck. Try hard, because I think that big guy has everything. He could develop into a really good pitcher."

When Hayes arrived in Orlando and started asking around about Sam Jones, the word leaked out and the manager of the local hotel team tried to block the signing, but everything worked out okay.

Wilbur Hayes did a bang-up job of delivering the goods.

Chet Brewer was our pitching coach that year, and I turned Sam over to him. Chet was known for having a curve ball that wouldn't quit, and I had visions of the Buckeyes being Negro League Champs again if he could just teach that curve ball to Sam.

◆ ◆ ◆

The following year, 1948, we did win another pennant, and we went into the play-off series against the New York Cubans to play for the Negro League Championship.

We played our first game at Yankee Stadium, and Campanella and his wife were in the stands.

"Hi, Roy," I greeted him before the start of the game. "Ruth, you're as beautiful as ever."

"Quincy, how is everything?" Roy asked.

"Well, it could be worse," I said. "Are you through playing already? How did you make out up there in Nashua?"

"Oh, I did okay. We got into the playoffs."

"Quincy, luck to you today in the series," Ruth said, getting in a word.

"Thanks, Ruth. Hey, Roy, would you take a few shots of the game with my movie camera?"

"Sure," Roy said.

I gave him the camera, and then went out to home plate to get the ground rules.

After a while the game got underway. The Buckeyes won by a pretty big margin.

After the game, I went to get my camera from Roy. He and Ruth were waiting at the edge of the dugout. "Did you get me when I made that double?"

"Now, wait, Quincy! Don't get sore with me, man, but I was eating a hot dog when you got the two-base hit. I didn't get a thing."

"Aw, man!" But my disappointment couldn't last long. Roy and Ruth were always good company. "Wait for me, and we'll have dinner together."

"Fine, Quincy. We'll wait at the exit for you," Roy agreed.

The next day our teams moved to Philadelphia for our second game, which was rained out. We went on into Chicago, and from there to Cleveland.

As things turned out, we only managed to win one game against the New York Cubans, and they became the Negro League Champions for the first time in more than twenty years.

◆ ◆ ◆

The following winter I went to Puerto Rico to play, and a short time after the season began the manager resigned and the job was offered to me.

I turned it down at first, because the owners and several of their friends had sat in our dugout during the games second guessing everything the manager did.

I asked that no one be allowed on my bench except the players, coaches, and trainer. I put that condition for accepting the job into writing. It was agreed to at a board meeting, and I took the job.

One coach was released and another hired.

My pitching was beefed up with the signing of two players from the States.

I also brought Piper Davis down from the States to play second base, and signed Sam Bankhead for shortstop.

Next we picked up a young player to play first base; people in Puerto Rico called him Victor Pellot. He was great with the glove, but a weak hitter. I worked with him, and before the season was over his hitting was very respectable. When he came to the States he became known as Vic Power.

Our team jelled so well we went into the playoffs, and even though we were the underdogs our spirit was high.

We stood up there against them toe-to-toe and battled all the way down the line. Now we were in the final inning, with just one out to go before the opposition became champions.

I had been batting right-handed against a left-handed pitcher and he had gotten me out every time. If he got me out now, it would mean the team manager would have gone hitless on four trips to the plate and made the final out that would cost our club the championship.

It was do or die. I switched over to my left, even though I was batting against a left-handed pitcher, throwing away the book because there was one thing in this situation the book didn't cover—the right-field fence was only 320 feet away down the line.

We battled through a count of one and one, and then he fired a fast ball at the inside corner. I swung, laying into it with solid wood.

The ball sailed out over the right-field fence, and the game went into extra innings.

In the top half of the tenth, Power came to bat and doubled to left. I put in a runner for him. A bunt and hit produced a run. Perucho Cepeda went in to pinch hit and, with our fans cheering him on, came through with an infield hit that brought in the winning run.

PLAYERS I DEVELOPED IN THE U.S.A.

This was one of the greatest days of my baseball life. The people of the town made me Honorary Mayor for a day, and because I always loved children, I declared the day a holiday, closing down all the schools in town.

I was feted by the townspeople for a week before they would allow me to leave. Caguas, Puerto Rico, was just a small town, but the fans of baseball had something special for me every moment of the time they were my hosts.

I shall never forget their hospitality.

In '48 I was traded by the Cleveland Buckeyes to the Chicago American Giants.

Before leaving Puerto Rico, I contracted some Puerto Rican players for my new club.

During spring training I drove from Memphis to Asheville, West Virginia, twice and finally convinced Jim Pendleton to sign a contract.

After breaking camp we played several exhibition games all the way down to New Orleans. The Chicago American Giants were a very young team, but we showed a lot of promise.

The day we were leaving New Orleans, a player on another club asked me to let a young fellow go with us to Chicago. I agreed, and told him he would have to help us pack and watch the bus at night while we were playing—the boys had been leaving all of their money and watches in the bus, locked in a strong box. Everything was all right until we reached Nashville.

That night, after the game, the young guy we had fed, paid room rent for, and treated like a brother took off with the box, and we never saw him again.

Some of the boys lost as much as a hundred dollars.

One night we played Birmingham, and in the twelfth inning, with Jim Pendleton on base, I won the game with my second home run.

After the game I was sitting in a café eating when an old-time ball player came in and pulled up a chair. "Say, Trouppe, there is a young boy with the local team you ought to see. Boy, he can throw the ball from the center-field fence all the way home, and plays like he was born out there."

"Well, I always like to see any good young player. Where is he now?"

"You can find him upstairs in the hotel where you're staying. Just ask at the desk and they'll tell you his room."

"Okay, thanks. I'll see him."

At the hotel, after talking to the clerk, I knocked on the door of his room. "Come in."

Opening the door I saw a young guy, around 16, on the bed. "Are you Willie Mays?"

"Yes," he replied. He was not too big, but I noticed he had large hands and his frame indicated he was going to be a good-sized man.

"Someone told me you're interested in playing pro ball."

"I sure am!" Willie said.

"How would you like to have a tryout with the Chicago American Giants?"

"Well, I would really like to. But I'm not allowed to sign a contract myself.

You will have to talk to my daddy. I'm going home tomorrow, and I'll tell him about it."

"Well, okay. You have him get in touch with me in Chicago, and I'll send your expense money so you can join us there."

The next day we left for Chicago and played a few more games en route.

When we arrived in the Windy City all the players rushed to the office to get their mail. There was a letter for me from Fairfield, Alabama. After reading it, I handed it over to the team's owner, saying. "Mr. Martin, this is from a young boy I'd like to try out. I haven't seen him perform yet, but I'd like to very much."

The owner looked at the letter a few minutes and then asked, "How much is this he wants?" as though the amount wasn't there in the letter.

"Three hundred dollars," I replied.

"Mr. Trouppe, don't you think three hundred dollars is too much to advance to a player you have never even seen play?"

"Well, that is a lot of money, but he could turn out to be a real good ball player."

"I'm sorry Mr. Trouppe. I can't see myself sending that $300 to somebody you haven't seen play. I can't agree with you that Willie Mays is worth that much." He was very emphatic.

Two weeks later Chicago played Birmingham in Springfield, Illinois, and I saw young Willie in action that night for the first time. I hit a line drive to center field, and I just knew I had two bases, and maybe three if I hustled.

I was running hard down the second baseline when the shortstop, Artie Wilson, told me to hold up.

"The center fielder's got the ball," he said.

Man, oh man, what a prospect. And the Chicago American Giants had let him go by. I just shook my head.

When we got to New York the Dodgers were making a home stand, and I got to see Roy play.

He asked me to wait under the stands after the game. I did and found Ruth there waiting also. We took a taxi to a restaurant on 125th Street.

During dinner I asked Roy how he liked playing in the big league.

"Quincy," he said, "this is easy baseball. Naturally, for a youngster it would be hard, but for players like you and me—it's easy, man!"

At the tail end of the season, my young players had begun to pick up some experience and the team started to come around. We defeated Indianapolis in a double header, and in one of those games I connected in the pinch for a home run with the bases loaded.

We closed the season in Chicago and all the boys went home, figuring next season we would be fighting for the pennant.

10
CATCHING SAL MAGLIE AND MAX LANIER

In 1949, I was looking forward to managing another championship team when the owner of the Chicago American Giants, John Martin, informed me he had sold Jim Pendleton to the Brooklyn Dodgers. Then he floored me with a request that I take a cut in salary. Martin's logic was very peculiar. I had been the leading hitter on the team that year, and I was looking forward to a raise! So, I ended up getting traded to the New York Cubans.

I again played winter ball in Puerto Rico, bringing Gene Baker, Piper Davis, and Dan Bankhead over to play with me. My team finished second against some stiff competition, and I won a trophy for being the most valuable player in a league in which fans regularly came out to see top-ranked stars such as Bob Thurman, Willard Brown, and Luke Easter.

That same year the Caribbean series was inaugurated, opening in Havana, Cuba. The countries represented were Cuba, Puerto Rico, Venezuela, and Panama. I was one of the players chosen to represent Puerto Rico, and Monte Irvin and Sam Jethroe were the big guns for the Almenderes team from Cuba.

During the play-offs in Cuba I was approached to play ball in Canada. I had to decide between going to Canada or becoming the player-manager of the New York Cubans.

I returned home before making a decision, and when I arrived a telegram awaited me from Maracaibo, Venezuela, offering a contract.

On the drive up to Canada, I stopped on the road several times trying to decide if I really was doing the right thing. But when I got to visualizing the hot climate in South America, I became convinced that Canada was the right place to go.

I arrived in Drummondville, Quebec, Canada, one morning at around eight o'clock. I went to a café to have breakfast, but no one could understand a word I said—they all spoke French, a language I did not know. I became so disgusted with the whole idea that I just turned around and went back to the U.S. without letting anyone know I had ever been in Drummondville.

On my way back to St. Louis, I stopped in Columbus, Ohio. I thought it would be a good thing to let the team manager know I had decided not to play, so I checked into a hotel, had dinner, and then placed a call to the team's owners.

I talked to one of the co-owners for a minute or two, and then suddenly Max Lanier's voice sounded off.

He explained a lot of things to me, telling me there were many people who could speak English in Canada. And he told me about American players on the team. There was Sal Maglie, Danny Gardella, Roy Zimmerman, Joe Tuminelli, and himself.

Max painted the picture in such a beautiful manner that I headed back across the border.

The team needed a center fielder and a pitcher. I recommended Vic Power and Roberto Vargas, and they joined us about two weeks later. Our team started out in first place and stayed there all season.

During that period I found out that Max Lanier and Sal Maglie, our two pitching aces, had very different personalities. Max was very calm and an easy pitcher to catch. He never got nervous, and he could use the most complicated signals. Anytime Max Lanier had his control, he was a hard man to beat.

Someone told me later that Max had a sore arm during that time, but he certainly never showed it during the summer of '49. He pitched great ball for us right up until the time he rejoined the St. Louis Cardinals.

Sal was somewhat the opposite of Max. He didn't like to use complicated signals, preferring the simple kind. Sal also became nervous at times, especially when a game was close.

Once, when the three of us were talking about changing our signals and Max said it was okay with him, Sal protested.

"Look, Max, you and Trouppe can use any kind of signal you like, but I'll use the most simple ones. I don't care if they do know what's coming."

A little past the middle of the season, organized baseball reinstated Max Lanier and Sal Maglie. Sal went to New York for a few days and made arrangements to stay on with Drummondville for the remainder of the season.

One day a couple of strangers asked me a few questions as to whether or not Sal had enough going to win in the major leagues. I told them that Sal could win in anybody's league. "He has more natural stuff than Max Lanier, I think. Max has more know-how, that's all."

They wrote a few notes, thanked me, and left.

Maybe Sal never thought about it, but they say most outstanding pitchers have good catchers throughout their careers.

I talked to Sal about a basic way to pitch that came naturally with his style of delivery.

All pitchers can't throw the same pitch to a hitter. There are some pitchers who can get a certain batter out with his curve, while another pitcher can throw the same batter a curve and the infielder would need shin guards. Anyway, Sal had the necessary know-how to earn his reputation as "the Barber" the next year when he joined the New York Giants.

We ended our season in a play-off with Farnham. The series went seven games, and Drummondville barely managed to win the deciding game in the last inning by one run. Dave Pope was one of the hitting stars of the series in the lineup for Farnham.

◆ ◆ ◆

That year, 1949, Dorothy's divorce suit against me became final. I remember being very sad when I got the papers. Boy, did I love that little woman. Now I was a single man again, though, and there were plenty of fine young ladies to go around.

In the winter season of 1949-50, I received an offer to play in Aguadilla, Puerto Rico. The team had another American catcher, and while the manager and owner were trying to come to a decision, I made contact with a team in Cuba that definitely wanted me to play.

During a wait for transportation to Cuba, I had a talk with one of my young teammates, Johnny Logan, who told me he was having a bad season in hitting. "Johnny," I told him, "there have been good ball players sent home for having a better season than you are having at present, but let me say just one thing—don't ever give up. Fight all the way and let the manager or the owner decide on sending you home. Keep fighting, and you'll do all right."

"Well, Trouppe," he replied, "I guess you're right, but I know I could do better if only I could break out of this hitting slump."

"It could be that it's because you've never been out of the country before. It always makes a difference when you're playing with a foreign team. After you get used to everything, you'll be okay," I assured him.

Johnny thanked me and said that he would stick it out.

Later that season, while I was in Cuba, I read that Johnny Logan was rated the outstanding shortstop in Puerto Rico.

Willie Mays came to Cuba to play, but after he arrived, his team received a cable from the New York Giants saying he could not play. They kept him all season, anyway.

I didn't do bad that season myself; I was selected for the all-star team. However, I can't really claim I was a manager's delight. One day, while taking my turn during batting practice, I hit one back through the middle, catching the team's manager. He was hospitalized with a fractured ankle.

The next two years, 1950-51, I went to Mexico as a player-manager. The league was set up to play a split season. My team did not do too well in the first half, so I returned to the States and signed Piper Davis and Bill Greason.

Davis really helped defensively at second, and he held his own at the plate. In the play-offs, Davis hit one of the longest home runs I've ever seen in the Torreon Park.

Greason won eleven games that season and lost only one. His pitching was a key factor in our team rising to the top, and he won two out of the three games he pitched in the play-offs.

11
THE CLEVELAND INDIANS AND THE END OF THE LINE

After returning from Mexico in October 1951, I made a special trip to Chicago to talk with Abe Saperstein.

It was my understanding that he might be in a position to get a ball player on with a team in organized baseball. Abe told me to go on and play winter ball, and that he would see what was in the making that next spring.

Well, one day while relaxing in the hotel lobby in Caracas, Venezuela, with Jim Pendleton and Piper Davis, the bellboy gave me a message saying I had a long distance call. I didn't have the slightest idea who would be calling me.

The operator told me the call was from Cleveland, Ohio, and then I heard her speaking to the other party. "Mr. Greenberg, I have Mr. Trouppe on the line."

The voice came through very clearly. "Hello, Quincy. Hank Greenberg of the Cleveland Indians. How are you? What kind of a season are you having?"

I was so surprised I could hardly find words to answer him. I felt like I was fumbling. "Oh, hello, Hank. I'm okay and having a pretty good season."

Hank got right to the point. "Quincy, you have been recommended to the Indians, and I'd like to have you go to spring training with us. How would you like that?"

"You mean go to spring training with the Cleveland Indians?"

"Yes. Go to Tucson, Arizona, to train with the Cleveland Indians."

I was out of words.

Hank broke the momentary silence. "What I have decided to do, Quincy, is send you an Indianapolis contract, but it will be up to you to make the Cleveland team."

"Well, Hank, thanks a lot. This is the opportunity I've been waiting for for the last twenty years."

"Okay, Quincy. I'll send you a small bonus and the contract for you to sign and return to me."

"Thanks again, Hank. It was nice talking to you." Nice! Man, what an understatement that was.

"Okay, Quincy. See you in spring training."

◆ ◆ ◆

I finished with a good season in Venezuela. There were several Venezuelans anxious to play ball in the United States, and I recommended Chico Carrasquel's brother to the Indians.

In the spring of '52 I made the team.

I had really gotten myself into excellent condition. I was in the best shape I had been in for years, and I was ready to play ball, but once the regular season started I was sent to the bullpen.

Still, I guess no one who has ever broken into organized ball could have felt any better than I did when I inked my name to that new Cleveland Indians contract.

When our team was in Cleveland most of the extra players would go to the park early in order to get in extra batting practice, because we could never get in more than three to six swings when we were on the road. I only saw action in three games in two-and-a-half months. The rest of the time I sat on the bench— not the easiest thing to do when you're thirty-eight years old and accustomed to starting and running the show. After a while I found myself growing a little stale.

One day, while taking our preliminary workout before the game in Cleveland, Hank Greenberg sent word for me to see him in Lopez' office.

When I entered the office, Greenberg was seated at Lopez' desk, and he greeted me this way: "Hello, Quincy. Have a chair. I don't know exactly how to say it, but I'm afraid I have bad news for you. We have decided to send you down to Indianapolis."

This hit me with such force that I was speechless for a few minutes. Greenberg saw how it affected me, and he spoke up again. "Quincy, I want you to know that I feel that you should be our second catcher. I've even talked to Lopez, but he won't go along with the idea. Well, you understand. He is the manager, and there are certain things that we can't do over his head."

The terrible disappointment nearly choked me. I finally said, "Well, look, Hank. I don't think I'm being treated right."

Hank interrupted before I could say more. "Quincy, one thing you don't have is a record that we can go on."

He must have forgotten what he had said to me one day in Tucson. We were just about to start our morning session when he stopped me near the dugout to say, "Quincy, Campanella recommended you very highly. He thinks you can be a great help to the Indians this summer."

In replying to that, I told him, "All I want is a chance to show what I can do."

"Don't worry," Hank said. "You'll get the chance."

Then, later on, when I was signing my contract to become a Cleveland Indian, Hank told me, "Quincy, don't worry about a thing. You'll be here all season long."

He must have forgotten that, too.

Now he was talking about me not having a record to go on, and I was thinking about how I had caught every third game during spring training and gotten twice as many hits as the other two catchers, Hegan and Tebbetts. I thought about our exhibition game in Los Angeles, when I caught Early Wynn for seventeen straight scoreless innings until Eddie Robinson ended the string with a home run off a change-up pitch. I thought about the hit-and-run play I had anticipated the competition pulling in another game, when I called for a pitch-out and nailed the runner trying to go to second base. I thought about the Oakland, California, club in the Pacific Coast League trying to make a deal for me, and Indianapolis holding on like I was new money. I thought of the shutout I had caught for Bob Feller.

Bob's fast ball was no longer smoldering, and his curve ball, while big, didn't really have that snap. But his control was still superb, and with his reputation and intelligence I felt if he used a change of pace and mixed up his pitches, his fast ball could still get by when he cut loose.

I suggested this to Bob, and he pitched a shutout.

The next day, while I was in the outfield shagging flies, Bob came over and told me, "Quincy, you called a very good game yesterday. You really used excellent judgment on the hitters, and you also knew how to use my most effective pitch. Keep up the good work."

"Thanks a million, Bob. Such a compliment coming from you means a lot to me," I replied. It did, too.

I thought about Larry Doby, Luke Easter, Harry Simpson, Bob Kennedy, and Mel Harder telling me about what a good job I was doing and how glad they were to have me as part of the gang.

And then I was back on that St. Louis street corner, a twelve-year-old kid, dreaming about playing major-league baseball while listening to the voice of Dick Kent on the megaphone yelling out which way the foul balls were heading before they appeared over the roof and landed on Compton or Market Street. The ball chasers Kent had hired to take balls off of the kids never had to worry about me—those balls were my free ticket into the park, and I lived to see those games.

I thought of all the highs and all the lows that went into putting together twenty-two years of playing ball on two different continents and islands in between; of the too many, too often hello–good-byes; of the big hotels, the jets, the cities strung out in lights below while I winged through the sky; of the looks in the eyes of children pressing me for an autograph; of the excited way the St. Louis Stars' fans got to pounding their soda-water bottles on the wooden stands until those old wooden benches were rocking as they tried to start a rally; of the guy who always climbed to the top of the wire screen every time Mule Suttles sent one sailing out of the park; and of winning the championship in four straight games my first year out as player-manager. I thought about it all, a thousand and one things that spelled out my quest for a golden American dream that was now collapsing under the razor-edged reality of Hank Greenberg's voice telling me that because I didn't have a record playing in organized ball I had to return to their minor-league farm club.

THE CLEVELAND INDIANS AND THE END OF THE LINE

"Hank, look," I said. "You saw what I did in spring training. Do you have to have a record of a man to determine what he can do? You saw me in action. What else is necessary?"

Hank's voice developed a consoling note. "Well, Quincy, I'll tell you what I'll do. You go down to Indianapolis and do a good job. Make a good record, and I'll bring you back."

"Hank," I said, "I feel that I've done a good job. There are others who think so, too. I don't know what the manager thinks, because he has never held a conversation with me to learn anything about me. You see, in the many years I've played baseball and managed, I always found it absolutely necessary to talk with my players to learn what they think and feel. Hank, I don't feel I deserve this demotion."

"Now, Quincy, don't feel like that about it. There is another reason I'd like you to go down to Indianapolis, and that is to work with our young pitchers. We have several promising young prospects. I'd like you to work with Herb Score, Ray Narleski, Zuverink, and some others. The team is away now, but they will be home this coming Sunday. Be sure and meet them there."

Hank got up, shook my hand, and said, "Good luck, Quincy. Like I said, go on down there and do a good job and everything will be okay."

I was so let down I didn't return to the field at all, but went straight to the club dressing room. I didn't want to talk or do anything, just be alone. Some of the fellows came in and changed sweatshirts, but I hardly knew they were there. I changed clothing, got all my baseball equipment, and returned to the room where I was living with a private family.

◆ ◆ ◆

Even though I was keenly disappointed, life had too much to offer for me to become bitter and bury myself in loneliness.

I had, a short time prior to my talk with Greenberg, become engaged to Myralin Donaldson, a marvelous young woman from New Orleans whose beauty was enhanced by a wonderful sense of humor.

After deciding to go to Indianapolis, I asked her to join me there and become my wife.

We made arrangements for her to follow me two weeks after my arrival, and she and I were married with Al Smith as best man.

Marriage was great, and during my first two weeks with the Indianapolis club I hit six home runs. I began to think I might get another chance until I read in the newspaper that Cleveland had bought Tipton to help out in the catching department. I guess you can imagine how that made me feel.

Everything seemed to go down the drain after that as far as baseball was concerned. The other catcher on the Indianapolis team got hurt, and I had a bad knee. But there was one good thing I did have, and that was my wonderful wife.

Two days after the close of the season, Al Smith and I drove to St. Louis.

"Smitty," I told him, "I got to the majors, if just for three months. You have a good chance to make it up there, but you've got to lose that stomach. You're too fat to give a good account of yourself."

"Yes, I know," he admitted. "I've been sore because I don't think I've been given a good shot. But that's in the past now. I'm going to spring training next year and win myself a job. You know, I hit twenty home runs, but they didn't call me up at the end of the season."

"Just remember what I've said about your weight and you'll make it," I told him.

We drove to St. Louis in six hours and stayed a couple of weeks making preparations to play winter ball.

One day Smith called me from his home and asked me for a couple of bats. I told him that if I was out when he came by my mother would give them to him.

"Where are you going this year, Quincy?"

"Back to Venezuela. Myralin will be here in a couple of weeks. She's going with me. How about you?"

"I'm going to Ponce, Puerto Rico. I don't know if Betty is going with me. We haven't decided yet."

"Well, have a good year down there, and good luck!"

"Thanks, Quincy. The same to you."

Before leaving St. Louis, just like always, I went to see Sam Bennett, an old gentleman who had inspired me through the years with his wealth of tips and advice.

We would sit across a table from one another in his sitting room, and he would explain every phase of early baseball and describe the great Negro players in the days of his youth. He painted the pictures so vividly it was like listening to a game over the radio.

He told me how Bingo De Moss could stand up there at the plate without them being able to tell when he was going to bunt, because he would never square around like the average batter. Many times old-timers bunted after taking two strikes. They were so good that not only did they drag and push the ball, but they could also bunt it almost anywhere they wanted to.

"When De Moss made the double play, he hardly ever looked directly toward first base. He could make the play by a half glance," Sam said.

In Sam's day a batter became a better hitter by becoming a better bunter. Guys like De Moss, Jimmy Lyons, Frank Warfield, Oscar Charleston, Joe Hewitt, Bobby Williams, Jelly Gardner, Cool Papa Bell, and Dave Malarcher were masters at this.

Most batters back then choked the bat a little. The sluggers were the only ones who held the bat at the end. A batter can guide his bat better if he chokes it a little. Most ball players during those days could really duck, and if the pitch was too close around the body they would move away just far enough to keep from taking the full impact of the ball, and get awarded first base by the ump for being hit by it.

"We never really tried to hurt anyone, but there were times when guys did get hurt. If a pitcher knew a certain player could not get out of the way of a pitch, it would not be thrown at him. On the other hand, they threw hard at batters they knew could duck," Sam said.

He showed me a 1921 clipping of a game between the Chicago American Giants and the St. Louis Giants (the St. Louis Giants changed their name to the Stars later that year). Chicago won the game 1-0; St. Louis only got two hits, both in the ninth inning.

Dave Brown was the pitcher for Chicago, and Plunk Drake for St. Louis. The only run scored in the game came in the eighth inning on a squeeze play with Torrienti on third and Gardner laying down a perfect bunt.

"Son," Sam said, "when I was playing baseball, we practiced hard on every phase of the game. Fellows could slide, run bases—oh, they did everything well, including think. Take Plunk Drake. He had good control, good stuff on the ball, and he was smart."

I asked him about Rube Foster and Jim Taylor. I had seen Taylor manage.

"Well, son, Rube was one of the smartest. He knew what his men could do, and he always found out the weakness of the competition. I tell you, Quincy, to play for Rube you either had to be smart with ability, or you had to have some extra talent."

"What about Taylor?"

Sam closed the scrapbook, which had been open on the table in front of us. "Jim was a good man, but not as good as Rube. He was at his best when it came to developing young ball players. He had a way with them that really brought out their best."

"Sam, what about when you fellows played big-league all stars?"

"Back in my day we played the regular team. If it was the Dodgers, it would be their whole team, or the Cardinals, or whoever. They might have one, or maybe two guys playing with them who weren't on their regular squad."

"How did you come out?"

"Oh, I guess altogether we broke even. We beat them and they beat us."

"Well, Sam," I said, getting up and moving toward the door, "it's always good talking to you. I'm going to South America in a week, so if I don't see you any more this year I'll check in with you in March. Take care of yourself."

He walked me to the door and wished me luck. I could tell it gave Sam a lift spending time talking about something he loved as much as he loved baseball.

Myralin and I flew to New York, but she became ill on the plane and could not enjoy the trip. While we waited in New York for our passports, her health improved; when we arrived in Caracas she was feeling good, but after a few days she became ill again. A few weeks before Christmas we decided it was best for her to return home, especially since she was pregnant.

I had a good season that year in Venezuela, and was runner-up in home runs.

12
SCOUTING FOR THE
ST. LOUIS CARDINALS

In the spring of '53 I really did not know whether I wanted to play baseball anymore or hang it up.

George Tebbetts, the manager at Indianapolis, gave me permission to go home and think it over.

While I was home I applied to scout for two ball clubs and called a friend who was playing ball in the Dominican Republic. He urged me to go with him, and I got an offer as a player that was too good to refuse.

The Dominican Republic was not in organized baseball. At that time, the teams were in spring training, and most of the top officials were there.

When I arrived, Luis Olmo and Bert Haas were there. Guaybin Olivo and his brother were also on the team.

After training for three weeks, I received a telegram from St. Louis regarding my scouting application.

I returned home, and after consultation with chief scout Joe Mathes and owner August A. Busch, I was hired to scout for the St. Louis Cardinals.

After being hired, I asked my supervisor if it would be all right to scout the schools in the New Orleans area for a few weeks. He gave me the green light, and I left St. Louis for New Orleans, where Myralin was staying with her family.

Myralin's grandmother, affectionately known as "Big Mama," headed a warm, friendly family that included my wife, her sisters, Lota and Evelyn, and her parents, Walter and Lucille Donaldson. They lived in a large residence that had been converted into a two-family duplex. The back doors of each duplex practically opened into each other, and it was easy for everybody to gather in Big Mama's kitchen for morning coffee. Morning coffee was the big event of the day.

Myralin's father, whom she always called by first name, was in charge of making the coffee for the family. She insisted no one could make creole coffee as good as her father could, and although I am not a coffee drinker, I am convinced she was right.

Walter Donaldson took special pleasure in preparing that coffee; he always took the first cup to his wife, who drank it in bed while reading the morning paper. One morning she called my attention to an article in the paper stating that the Kansas City Monarchs were to play the next day at the Pelican Stadium.

The Monarchs, managed by Buck O'Neal, who I knew very well from my ball-playing days in North Dakota, were playing a local team. Buck's team traveled around playing ball all over the country.

It took me only a little while to locate Buck at his hotel, and we had such a long talk about old times I almost forgot I had dropped by to ask about his team.

The first man he mentioned was Ernie Banks. "Trouppe," he said, "I got a horse and you better jump on him; ride him, now. If you don't, someone else will."

He told me the boy was not with the team at that moment, but was joining the next day.

I sent a report at once to the office in St. Louis, recommending the signing of Banks on the word of Buck O'Neal.

◆ ◆ ◆

On May 13, 1953, my wife gave birth to a seven-pound girl, Stephanie Marie. We felt blessed by God since we had both wanted a daughter.

I spent the first few days of Stephanie's life taking movies of her. She was a beautiful baby, and we were very proud parents.

After making contact with the coaches in the high schools and at Xavier University, I started working my way back toward St. Louis, routing my schedule to pass through Memphis on a Sunday in order to see Ernie Banks play.

There is something about the actions of a ball player that lets you know whether he has what it takes to really be a star. Banks did not hit that day, but he showed excellent wrist action. His reflexes were very smooth, and he had a good throwing arm.

Through the years I have found that most of the great ball players I have known are relaxed people, like Josh Gibson. Many others, such as Willie Wells, Oscar Charleston, Jud Wilson, Ray Dandridge, and Martin Dihigo, have fit this pattern. I think if a man has this kind of personality, plus ability, his chances are far above average. Ernie Banks was all of this the first time I saw him play.

When I arrived in St. Louis, my first thought was to find out about my report on Banks. I found that another scout had been sent to look at him right after my report was received, and did not like him. It seemed the organization was going to go along with that scout's judgment.

One morning I got to the office in time to join in on a conversation about Ernie Banks. The scout who had given the negative report said, "I don't think he is a major-league prospect. He can't hit, he can't run, he has a pretty good arm, but it's a scatter arm. I don't like him."

Taking a chair next to the supervisor's desk, I spoke up. The chief scout, the minor-league supervisor, and the supervisor's assistant were all there at their desks listening. "Well, I like Ernie Banks, and I think with a little polishing he can play major-league ball."

Then I told the scout who didn't like Banks that I had no hard feelings toward him. I knew it was his job to give an honest opinion, just as it was mine.

"Quincy, you keep a check on Banks and let me know more about him during the season. Right now, I want you to join Frank Crespi and learn how to operate a tryout camp," Mathes said.

Tryout camps were held all through the New England states. During this trip I met a Cardinal scout by the name of Bennie Borgin. "Quincy, in my opinion, the greatest ball player I've ever seen was Oscar Charleston," he told me. "When I say this, I'm not overlooking Ruth, Cobb, Gehrig, and all of them."

After two weeks with the tryout camp, I returned to St. Louis to take up my regular scouting duties. I kept a check on the Kansas City Monarchs every time they played in the vicinity.

Banks was to play in the big East-West game in Chicago that year, and my supervisor made arrangements to see him play, too.

The owner of the Monarchs asked me why I had not recommended Ernie Banks to the Cardinals. I told him I had, and he advised me that Chicago was interested in him too.

Banks was not outstanding in the East-West game, and my supervisor asked me to follow the Monarchs for another week and make a report to him.

I followed them down through the southeast and back to Louisville, Kentucky. There I got a telephone call from St. Louis, at 9:00 a.m., asking me to report to the home office immediately. At 3:30 that afternoon, I was in the Cardinal's office.

My supervisor asked me to come back in the morning to have a meeting with Eddie Stanky, who was managing the Cardinals that year.

At the morning meeting, Stanky asked, "Quincy, do you know of two colored ball players who could play on the Cardinals?"

That was a big question, and I finally answered, "Well, Eddie, the only two players I'd recommend would be Vic Power and Ernie Banks, both now with the Kansas City Monarchs. Banks may need a little polishing, but I think he has everything." Stanky asked about Vic Power, wanting to know about his temperament and ability, which I certainly knew about after managing him for two years and playing on the same club with him one year in Canada.

"Power is ready right now to play on the Cardinals. He is a good hitter, good runner, excellent fielder, and his arm is adequate. Can you make a deal for him? You know he belongs to the Yankees?"

"I think we can deal for him," he replied. "Tell me one more thing, Quincy," Eddie said, pondering. "Does Vic Power like white girls?"

His shot landed solidly on my chin. He had caught me off guard, and I told him the truth. "Well, Eddie, Vic Power is a Puerto Rican, and matters of this sort don't make any difference in his country."

"Oh, well," Eddie said apologetically, "once he's on the team, I think I can handle everything." Then he asked, "What's the name of the fellow with the Monarchs?"

"Ernie Banks."

Eddie wrote the name on a piece of paper and the meeting was over.

Two weeks later the Chicago Cubs signed Ernie Banks.

I wonder if I had lied to the Cardinals about Power whether they would have hired him? But I'm sure he had been scouted by someone else, and that talk about white girls was in that scout's report.

Would I have lost my job if he had known how I feel about white women? As a matter of fact, I like white women, colored women, Japanese women, Chinese women, Mexican women, Latin women—oh, I like women, period. I don't care what color they are.

I recall the time in '49 when I had gone to Canada and turned around and headed back to the U.S. I had been in that little Canadian town long enough to notice that there were no people of my race there, and I did not like that either. Upon my return to Canada, after I was there a few weeks, I told my trainer, "Look, man, I hope you don't think I'm going to play ball the whole season here and not go out with a woman."

He was French-Canadian and cool as could be. "Don't worry. I'll introduce you to a girl," he told me.

He kept his promise. I met a very attractive young lady, and we had several dates. We went to beaches, clubs, even to Montreal.

One day while sitting on the beach she said, "There is an American player on your team I don't like."

I asked her who it was, and why she didn't like him.

Yolanda, a very pretty French-Canadian, directed her blue-eyed gaze at me and said, "I saw him here a few days ago, and he tried to date me. I told him I was already going out with a ball player. I told him it was you, Quincy. He said all kinds of bad things about you. He said that I shouldn't be going around with you. That I shouldn't date black men."

Naturally, I wanted to know who the player was, but she refused to say, telling me it would be best if I did not know.

To me, it seems unreal that a man's personal life, including his choice of women, can affect his career as long as he keeps it his own business and violates no law.

That same year of scouting for the Cardinals, I saw Pancho Herrera playing first base for the Kansas City Monarchs, and I sent in a card recommending him as a very good prospect.

One day I stopped by Cool Papa Bell's home, and we got to talking about old times and how the Negro had pioneered baseball into almost every country outside the United States. "Trouppe," he told me, "you were one of our best catchers. You could do everything. You could also play other positions well. You had a real good arm, were very fast, and were a good receiver. I think you were a better receiver than Josh. You could hit, and you had a deep knowledge of the game."

Any player likes to be thought of as good by another player, but coming from Cool Papa, what he had to say really meant something.

"Cool," I replied, "I've played in leagues with some of the guys they call great, and I've done some of the things they have done. I've been on the all-star team in every league I've ever played in. The only thing I can say is that my record speaks for me. I was a regular, twenty out of the twenty-two years I played pro ball. I've got a lifetime batting average that's way over .300. I batted against pitchers like Chet Brewer, Satchel Paige, Willie Foster, Pinky Powell, Henry McHenry, Bertrum Hunter, Martin Dihigo, Hilton Smith, Barney Morris, Billy Byrd, Terris McDuffie, Ruben Gomez, and others who had outstanding records in the many leagues I've played through the years. I know I held my own with the best."

"Most people who have been pretty close to baseball know that about you, Quincy," Cool responded.

"Well, Cool," I admitted, "I'm afraid I feel like an ex-ball player now."

Cool smiled. "He who hollers the loudest will be seen and recognized. I guess, Quincy, you just haven't hollered loud enough."

"Well, Cool, I guess that about sums it up."

One day when the New York Giants were in town I stopped by the clubhouse to see some of the fellows. While I was talking to Willie Mays about our days in Cuba, Ruben Gomez came up, slapped me on the back, and said, "Hi, Trouppe. I hear you are scouting now."

Shaking hands with Gomez, I told him, "Yeah, Ruben, I'm looking for prospects everywhere. Any young ones in Puerto Rico?"

Ruben replied, "Well, Trouppe, there is a young boy named Roberto Clemente. He is a very good prospect. You should go to Puerto Rico this winter and see him."

"I might just make the trip this fall."

"Well, he will play on the same team with me, and if you like him I don't think you will have any trouble signing him. You know Pedrin, the owner of my team?"

"Yes, I know Pedrin, he's a good friend. Okay, Ruben, I'll follow through on it. Thanks."

That fall I talked to my supervisor about going to Puerto Rico. He said the trip would have to be submitted to the general manager for approval.

The general manager gave me the go-ahead, and I took off.

When I arrived in San Juan, I found that scouts from several other organizations were there to see Clemente. I talked baseball awhile with Andy High, who was with the Dodgers.

Traveling around the island on several trips, I watched Clemente play. He was hitting against such pitchers as Bob Turley and Wehmeier.

Pedrin made arrangements for me to talk with Clemente and his father. We met in Pedrin's office. Clemente was anxious to sign with any organization, but his father was not so willing. After a lengthy talk, Clemente's father said that he would be willing to let the boy sign for a ten-thousand-dollar bonus, but that was the lowest amount he would accept.

My supervisor advised me to wait until I returned to St. Louis before making any commitments. When I got home, I made my report. In that report, I recommended giving Clemente the ten thousand dollars.

Four or five days passed, and in the meantime I received a cablegram from Clemente, asking me what was happening. I saw the general manager of the Cardinals the next day and asked him if I could get Clemente the ten-thousand-dollar bonus, and his answer was "No."

◆ ◆ ◆

Señor Garcia, owner of the Ponce Baseball Club in Ponce, Puerto Rico, contacted me about managing his team for the 1956-57 winter season, and after an exchange of letters, we came to an agreement. In my contract with Señor Garcia, I was to contract my own choice of players from the States.

Naturally, I tried to get as many boys out of the Cardinal organization as I could, but I was only able to get Tom Chenney and Barney Schultz.

I got most of my players from the Chicago Cubs through Wid Matthews. He really went out of his way to assist me in getting my team together, bringing me Steve Bilko, Jim Brosnan, Bob Speak, and Vito Valentinetti. I was able also to get Billy Harrell from the Cleveland Indians.

I thought I had a pretty good club with the players I had from the States and Puerto Ricans Luis Marquez, who had once played with the Braves, Carlos Brenier, who was with the Pirates, and several others who were playing A-league ball in the U.S.A.

Before the season started I had a meeting with the club explaining my system and how the signals worked.

No one had anything to say when I asked if there were any questions, so I believed everything was okay.

One particular thing I laid emphasis on was the take sign. I made it known that I didn't know any of the fellows, so I'd let them hit for themselves until further notice.

My team got off to a bad start. The pitching was good, but the hitters weren't carrying their weight.

Bilko had a great year on the Pacific Coast in '56, but he couldn't seem to get started in Puerto Rico. I don't know what happened, but none of my hitters seemed to be able to get going.

One day the owner held a meeting with my Americans and one or two of the Puerto Ricans. He wanted to know what the trouble was and why the team was not winning. I was told later that one of my American players said I had not done a good job managing. He said I had taken the bat out of his hands, meaning that I didn't let him hit the way he could hit best.

The owner, listening to the criticism by one of my countrymen, took action against me. I lost my job as manager, and I was really surprised when I found out it was Bob Speak who talked against me. I thought he was an all right guy.

A man is a man, however, no matter where he comes from, and I found friends in four players from different parts of the United States. Tom Chenney was from Morgan City, Georgia, and there wasn't a finer guy on my team. Steve Bilko was from Pennsylvania, and he, too, was a great guy to have around. Billy Harrell, from New York State, became a good friend, and he was the only American of my race on the team. Jim Brosnan and his wife also became good friends of mine.

It was too bad the owner couldn't have used better judgment.

◆ ◆ ◆

During 1957, the Cardinals made a change in personnel that put me under the supervision of another department, and I wasn't offered a contract for the following year.

One day I received a letter from my new supervisor, Walter Shannon, which asked that I report to the office right away. The letter spelled bad news, I knew. Usually when I was wanted in the office I received a telephone call.

When I was seated in Shannon's office at 10:00 the next morning he closed all the doors and then sat down at his desk. "Quincy, I've been talking with Frank Lane about you, and he feels the same as I do. We don't think you fit into our program, so we are not offering you a contract for next year. When does your contract terminate? October?"

Without bothering to wait for me to reply, he continued.

"Well, I'll add an extra month to tide you over until you can get something else."

His words, in reality, were not too much of a shock. I had sensed what was coming when I first saw the letter. "Walter, if that's the way you see it, there's nothing I can do. I'm sure you haven't forgotten the men I tried so hard to get for this organization—Ernie Banks, Roberto Clemente, Vic Power. . . ."

"Well," Shannon replied, "you know you must sign ball players, not just recommend them."

Shannon was just shooting double talk, and both of us knew it. Scouts only recommend players. The organization has to sign them.

I thought of when Shannon had been a scout like myself, before he got his big promotion, and how he and Monahan recommended thirty-seven thousand dollars for the signing of Dick Schoefield around the same time I could not get a ten-thousand-dollar bonus for Clemente.

"Walter," I asked, "what about the boys I have already signed who are playing in the minor league?"

He said in an indifferent manner, "Quincy, as I see the situation, you just don't fit into my program."

He suggested that I stop in at Bing Devine's office on my way out. Bing was assistant to Frank Lane, and he had always been a straight guy.

I turned in my stopwatch, bluebook, and a few other necessary articles that a scout is furnished with.

"Quincy?" said Bing, as I headed for the door.

I turned and he hesitated. His eyes were saying a lot, and the emotion came out in his voice, although all that he said was, "Be sure and call me anytime you want to go to a ball game."

A little later they retired Joe Mathes, and the public wrote so many letters into the office that it was decided to keep him on as a special scout. He had been with the Cardinals ever since Sam Breaden had owned the club, and the special-scout assignment was a cover-up to soothe the troubled waters they had stirred up letting him go.

Joe was really quite a guy. Once, after I recommended Vic Power to Eddie Stanky, Joe asked me about Power. In fact, he took me down to the office of August Busch, Jr., and had me tell him about Power's ability.

I remember when I first was hired into the organization and Joe asked me what was the right way to go about talking to colored people. I felt then it would be all right working with such a man, and I was right. He was one of the finest persons I ever worked for.

It was Harold Hummell who first pointed Joe Mathes out to me. Hummell had been very helpful in getting me my job with the Cardinals. "Joe Mathes is a man with whom you can feel at ease, Quincy. A person's nationality makes no difference to him. I'm sure you will have a friend in Joe Mathes. He's a wonderful human being."

I called Joe one day after I had been let go and asked if he would give me a letter of recommendation.

"Quincy," he replied, "you know I will. Anytime. And if you want anyone to call me, just give them my office or home number. Another thing, if I hear of anyone needing a man with your ability, I'll certainly recommend you. If I can do anything for you, Quincy, don't hesitate to get in touch with me." And then he added what he always used to tell me: "Hang in there, Quincy, and keep on pitching."

I must admit, I was pretty teed off about the curt way the organization had laid me off, but I had a real good feeling, and a lot of respect, for Joe Mathes.

Joe sent the letter of recommendation and promised to put in a good word for me with Gabe Paul if he ran into him at the league meeting being held in the Chase Hotel.

I took Joe's advice about getting in touch with new entry teams at the league meeting, and I called Gabe Paul. I had talked to him before when I was recruiting players for winter-league ball on the team I managed in Puerto Rico.

Gabe promised to get in touch with me if something opened up in his organization. I never heard from him. In fact, except for a few routine letters responding to my letters of inquiry, I heard nothing from organized baseball, and I wrote every club in the major leagues.

This says a lot about how many people think in the front offices of organized ball.

Most people will agree that the changes that have come about due to the integration of teams in organized baseball have been good.

However, there is another side of the coin. Once there was a time when talented men of color went to the Latin countries and got hired as managers, or coaches. Today, the front offices of organized ball seem determined to make those positions white men's jobs, and to a large extent they have succeeded.

Many people who make the decisions in the front offices still think lily-white, and this mentality has an adverse effect on the players competing on the diamond, and it lowers the level of performance the fans are paying to see.

Having firsthand knowledge of how insidious the influence of the front office can be, I can really appreciate Wid Mathews of the Chicago Cubs. I am certainly grateful to him for making it possible for me to get most of the players I had on my winter league team of '56-'57.

One day I was getting my hair cut in the Hollice Barbershop, owned by Richard Cooper and Thomas Burroughs.

Both Richard and Thomas had books on the history of baseball. They were very knowledgeable about it, and they loved to discuss the game.

Robert "Pro" Ewing, another friend of mine, was there also, and the topic finally drifted around to my not being with the Cardinal organization anymore.

"Trouppe," it was finally asked, "didn't you find any good boys in the five years you were scouting?"

What they were getting at was the fact that the Cardinals were still lily-white.

"I'd rather not talk about it," I said, "but, I will say this—a lot of people didn't know what part I played in the career of Vic Power until he was interviewed by one of the sports magazines. Sooner or later, time will tell the story."

"What are you going to do now? Are you going with another organization?"

"I don't think so. Although baseball is my first love, I'm going to look around for something I can depend on year in and year out."

I pulled my collar up around my neck, and the guys wished me well.

"See you fellows. Take it easy," I said, walking out the door.

Not long after that, my beloved mother succumbed to pneumonia. I don't mind saying that her passing hit me pretty hard.

After some phone calls and talking to some of my political friends, I got a job with the Land Clearance Authority, and I tried keeping my mind occupied with my work. The job was a very interesting one. I had to relocate families out of the Mill Creek area into other areas having standard housing quarters; this wasn't easy, because many of the families couldn't afford to pay standard housing rent. I remember when I first came to St. Louis housing conditions in many areas were deplorable, but here we were in the 1950s, and in spite of all the promises, not too much new was happening.

One day I came home to find some of Myralin's relatives from Cleveland, my wife's adopted city, in town for the weekend.

They asked me if she could go with them to Cleveland for a little visit.

Since Myralin had just returned from a trip to New Orleans with our daughter Stephanie, and I had missed them very much, I explained that I wanted her at home. Besides, we really could not afford another trip at this time, I told them. We had just purchased a new home, too, and I thought we ought to spend some time enjoying it.

Myralin, however, saw things differently. She insisted that there would be no additional expense involved in the trip.

Sal, who drove the car, said he would bring her back in a couple of weeks. Her relatives sided strongly with her, so, reluctantly, I agreed. "Well, Myralin, you'll need money, regardless. I only have a few dollars on me."

They were pushing to leave almost immediately, and I had to get to work.

"Quincy," Myralin said, "I don't need any money. I'll be with my relatives. It will be like living at home."

"Well, you'll need some, anyway. So stop by the office later, and I'll give you whatever I can get right away."

Just before noon they stopped at the office, and I went out to the car.

I will always remember my little daughter sitting in the front seat, just looking at me with her eyes so wide.

It was then I knew Myralin was leaving me and taking my Stephanie with her.

Words kind of stuck in my throat, but I managed to say, "Hi, sweetheart. So you are leaving your Daddy. I'm going to miss you. Be sweet. Be a good girl."

Myralin did not return to St. Louis, making all kinds of excuses. She got a job in Cleveland, finally, and sent Stephanie to New Orleans to stay with her mother. Anxious about the entire situation, I informed Myralin I was coming to Cleveland to see them, and she had her sister Lota bring Stephanie back to her for that occasion.

We signed property agreements and agreed to a divorce. Then I returned to St. Louis alone, and soon found that I could not tolerate living in our home. It held too many memories.

I moved into another place, but the memories were still around.

One day I received a letter from a friend in Los Angeles, telling me how nice it was in California. I had always thought of returning there someday to live, and right now, I realized, that time had come.

So I informed my supervisor of my plans and told him I'd like to resign.

He was really sorry to see me go. "You're my best man on relocation," he told me. "I don't know what I'm going to do without you."

I smiled, and thanked him for everything.

13
BACK IN BASEBALL

It was 1960, and I was driving to California. My particular joy at this time was my boys, with whom I have always kept in contact. They were in the army in Europe, and I was extremely proud of both of them.

Timothy is now a minister, and Quincy, Jr., is a writer and a very good one.

After arriving in Los Angeles I checked with a couple of old friends, and in a few weeks I went to work as an inspector at a manufacturing plant.

During my third year in Los Angeles I married Bessie Cullins, and my life took on a new and wonderful meaning. The boys love her very much, as does everyone who meets her. I have a family life that is very warm and fulfilling.

For a few years, Bessie and I owned and operated a very popular restaurant, called Trouppe's Dugout. It is a matter of fact that Bessie Trouppe is the most superb cook in the world. People literally come from all over the country with hopes of being guests at one of her meals.

It was while I was in the restaurant business that I started getting pressured on my job. My supervisor called me into his office one day and told me I would no longer be inspecting work in all the departments because a new job had been created for me.

Later on, after work, I thought it over and decided to take another shot at scouting. George Silvey, who was third man in the scouting department when I was in St. Louis, was now in charge. I knew George knew my ability, and I gave him a call.

George liked the idea of me scouting for the Cardinals in California and hired me immediately. The next day Harrison Wickel came into my restaurant with the contracts and I signed.

At work the next day, I went straight to the supervisor's office and told him I was resigning.

It really took him by surprise.

"But what will you do now, Quincy?"

"I've got a few things going."

He just couldn't get over it. A man of my age, resigning with jobs so hard to find.

"Now, Quincy, don't be hasty. I'm sure you will like the new job. We created it especially for you."

Our eyes met, and I said, "Look, you know, and I know, that this job you're talking about entails more heavy and physical work than I'm doing now. I'm sure you realize I'm not a youngster anymore."

"True, but you won't have to move around to all the departments like you have to do now."

Now we were getting down to the real issue. Management had resented me from the first day I was hired on as an inspector at the plant.

"Well," I told my supervisor, "I've talked everything over with my wife, and I'm going back into baseball scouting."

He just looked at me for a moment, then his expression started to sag. He forced a weak smile and said, "Boy, you're lucky. I'd like to have a job like that myself. Well, all I can say is, lot's of luck." I took his limp, extended handshake and left.

I scouted for the Cardinals until 1970, and Bobby Tolan, who has played for many major-league teams, is one of the players I recommended that the Cardinals did sign. I've thought many times about Roberto Clemente and Ernie Banks, both now in the Baseball Hall of Fame, and I am happy to see that they made it.

However, it is very disturbing that the selection committee voted into the Hall of Fame black ball players who never played in the majors. I disagree emphatically with their announcement that they are satisfied that their mission of voting all qualified black ball players into the Hall of Fame has been accomplished.

First of all, few people knew who the committee members were and what their qualifications were for judging the merits of ball players. Did they see all the black ball players play? What criteria did they use for picking players for the Hall of Fame? How did they go about determining who should be in it?

I agree that some of their selections would be on anybody's list, but there are some players named who I don't believe have the qualifications to be named as members of the Hall of Fame.

It would be a shame to forget men like Bizz Mackey, Christobal Torrienti, Joe Rogan, Joe Williams, Dick Redding, Willie Foster, Charlie "Chino" Smith, Chet Brewer, and Louis Santop, among others. I hope someday to get together with other concerned professionals and do something about starting another committee to ensure that deserving ball players are given their places in the Hall of Fame. And let's not wait another twenty years to get the job done. Let's do it now.

Satchel Paige organized this all-star team in 1946. Left to right: Hilton Smith, Kansas City Monarchs; Howard Easterling, Homestead Grays; Barney Brown, Philadelphia Stars; Sam Jethroe, Cleveland Buckeyes; Gentry Jessup, Chicago American Giants; Hank Thompson, Kansas City Monarchs; Max Manning, Newark Eagles; Othello Renfroe, Kansas City Monarchs; Rufus Lewis, Newark Eagles; Gene Benson, Philadelphia Stars; John O'Neil, Kansas City Monarchs; Frank Duncan, Kansas City Monarchs; Artie Wilson, Birmingham Black Barons; Quincy Trouppe, Cleveland Buckeyes. On the steps of the plane are Satchel Paige (right), his valet (left), and William "Dizzy" Dismukes, business manager. Courtesy Quincy Troupe, Jr.

Winter-league ball in Mexico and South America was an important part of many players' careers, allowing them to play virtually year-round. Here Quincy (back row, fourth from the left) poses with the 1946-47 Caraquas, Venezuela, Magallanes team. Some of the players pictured here had, or would have, important connections to baseball in other countries as well: Luis Aparicio (front row, fourth from the left) had a son of the same name who played shortstop for the Chicago White Sox and Boston Red Sox; Cuco Correa (front row, sixth from the left) was an outstanding second baseman in Cuba; Alexander Carrasquel (back row, fifth from the left) was the uncle of Chico Carrasquel, who played for the Washington Senators. Courtesy Quincy Troupe, Jr.

The East-West games were always exciting, as high caliber players had the opportunity to play with—and against—each other. Here Quincy (playing for the West) tags out his good friend Monte Irvin in Comiskey Park, Chicago, 1947. The West won 5-2. Courtesy Quincy Troupe, Jr.

Quincy reluctantly agreed to play and manage baseball in Canada in 1949. Despite his reservations, he led his team, the Drummondville, Quebec, Cubs, to capture the Provincial League championship that year. He receives congratulations from Drummondville's mayor in this photo. Courtesy Quincy Troupe, Jr.

The 1949 Drummondville, Quebec, Cubs. Left to right: Jerry Cotnoir, catcher; Roy Zimmerman, infielder; Roger Breard, infielder; Quincy Trouppe, catcher; Lennie Hoker, pitcher; Sal Maglie, pitcher; Conrado Perez, outfielder; Roberto Vargas, pitcher; Joe Prom, pitcher; Joe Tuminelli, infielder; Danny Gardella, outfielder; Stan Breard, infielder; Victor Pellot (Vic Power), outfielder; trainer. Courtesy Quincy Troupe, Jr.

In 1950 Quincy played for and managed the Guadalajara, Mexico, Jalisco team. The umpire has a close eye on the action in this photo, as Quincy, in his role as player, reaches for the play. Courtesy Quincy Troupe, Jr.

In his role as manager for Jalisco, Quincy strives to make the umpire see his point of view. Courtesy Quincy Troupe, Jr.

Yet another aspect of Quincy's baseball career outside of the United States: the 1951 Havana, Cuba, Marianao team. Tommy LaSorda, future manager of the Los Angeles Dodgers, is in the last row, second from the left. Back row, left to right: Antonio Garcia, pitcher; Tommy LaSorda, pitcher; Jose Mario Fernandez, Jr., catcher; Wesley G. Hamner, infielder; Damon Phillips, infielder; Sandalio Consuegra, pitcher; Gumersindo Elba, pitcher; Mario Diaz, catcher; unidentified rookie. Middle row, left to right: Roberto Estalella, trainer; Pedro Antonez, rookie; Archie Wilson, outfielder; Claro Duany, outfielder; Red Barrett, pitcher; Quincy Trouppe, catcher; Lorenzo Cabrera, first base; Rogelio Martinez, pitcher; Carlos Blanco, infielder; team doctor. Front row, left to right: Ray Dandridge, infielder; Orestes "Minnie" Minoso, outfielder; Amado Ibanez, infielder; Cando Lopez, coach; Adolfo Luque, manager; Jose Mario Fernandez, Sr., coach; Richmond, outfielder; James B. Pendergast, pitcher; Howard Moss, outfielder. Courtesy Quincy Troupe, Jr.

Quincy finally broke into the recently integrated major leagues when Hank Greenberg of the Cleveland Indians invited him for a tryout. He made the team in the spring of 1952, but was sent back to the Indians' farm club in Indianapolis after playing in only three games in two-and-a-half months. Courtesy Quincy Troupe, Jr.

Quincy Trouppe, Sr. Courtesy Quincy Troupe, Jr.

EPILOGUE

CATCHING TIPS

I'd like to mention catching to some of the young boys who think of it as being a position of hard work, and a bit dangerous. I do admit there is a considerable amount of work in catching, but the danger can be eliminated by learning the fundamentals of the position.

Playing twenty-two summer and twelve winter seasons, I never had a broken finger. I don't credit this to luck, but to the way I was taught to catch.

An old-timer named T. J. Young showed me how to hold my hands while receiving the ball. Young explained to me that most times a catcher gets hit on the hand by a fouled ball, the pitch is bad. When a good pitch is fouled, it either goes under or over the catcher's hand. For this reason, the catcher should always hold his hands parallel to the glove.

I was also taught how to shift on certain pitches. A catcher shouldn't move out or in before the pitcher pitches. In many cases, this will tip off the hitter as to where the pitcher is going to throw. Instead, he must be ready to move out when the ball is thrown outside. This is the case on either side of the plate, right or left.

A catcher must be agile on his feet, something like a boxer. When a boxer throws a left hook, usually he makes a little skipping shift. This is done most of the time when he leads with the left hook. This isn't always the case, especially when he counters with a left hook.

Similarly, a catcher has to shift with each pitch in order to be in a good position to throw to any base. If he is a right-handed thrower, he should always keep the left foot a little forward. The right foot should be forward if he is a left-handed thrower. However, as yet, we haven't had an outstanding left-handed catcher, but someday it may come to pass.

Another thing a catcher learns is to throw off the tip of his ear. That's the way I was taught. It allows him to get his throw off much faster.

The way I always caught a pop-fly ball up over the catcher's or batter's box was my own idea. I'm not sure what other catchers have thought about this, but I never had any trouble through twenty-two years in the game.

Catchers must remember that a ball travels in the direction in which it is spinning. When a ball is popped up over the catcher's head it is spinning in such a manner that it will fall in the direction of the pitcher's mound. I always moved out some three or four yards in front of home plate, with my back toward the pitcher's mound, because if any freak draft of wind should blow it away, I feel it is better to have a pop-fly ball drop in foul territory than in fair.

When the catcher is standing three or four yards in front of home plate, and the ball goes up over the plate, sometimes he has to move out into foul territory to catch the ball. But he must remember that the ball is spinning towards him. If he stands with his face toward the mound to catch the ball, the ball will travel away, into fair territory. If he doesn't catch up with it, and it falls fair, the batter is on base.

To get a quick jump on all pop-fly balls, the catcher makes a habit of looking straight up on any foul ball that pops up. If it is in playing territory, he can see it, and he will conserve his energy over a long period of time.

I've never had trouble tagging a man coming home. I don't believe in blocking the base unless the play is very close; I always figured it was better to take the throw up the line a little into fair territory. This will always give the catcher a chance to tag the man in plenty of time before he gets to home base.

This will also make him slide to one side, which is always less dangerous for the man making a tag. The only time that I've found it a bit dangerous tagging a man coming home is when he slides straight into the catcher. It is better to make him go to one side by getting up in front of home plate. When he slides straight in, all his weight is behind his spikes. When he slides to the side, there isn't much weight to worry about.

A catcher mustn't only be working harder physically than anyone else on the team throughout the game; he must also be thinking to his full capacity.

The first time I got behind the bat to catch, I found out that it was the most responsible position on the team.

One important thing I noticed was the direction in which the batter hit the ball. I noted where he hit the curve and the fast ball. Most batters have a tendency to hit the fast ball straight away or to the opposite side of the diamond, and to hit the curve to the same side of the diamond to which they are batting. This is true because a batter is usually swinging late on the fast ball, and as a result hits the ball straight away or to the opposite field.

For example, a right-handed batter hitting against a right-handed pitcher usually is pulling away from a curve. He pulls away because as the right-handed pitcher starts the curve, the batter has an instinctive tendency to move away from the ball. Consequently, he will pull the ball to that same side of the playing field.

One other thing a catcher has to think about is that usually a curve is thrown somewhat slower than the fast ball, so the batter has a chance to get around or out in front of this particular pitch. The same principle applies to left-handed hitters.

A catcher has to remember every batter in his league. He must remember what kind of pitch the batter hits hard. He has to remember the kinds of hitters (see Chapter 8). Some batters pull, some hit straight away, and others push the ball to the opposite field. Some swing up under the ball, some swing level, and others chop down. A catcher has to know why each of these batters hits most frequently to certain parts of the diamond. He also has to understand the angle or position the bat must be in when it meets the ball in order to hit it to a certain field.

Knowing these points, and knowing his pitcher, he will also understand how each hitter should be pitched to.

He should know that a pitcher with a good live fast ball can pitch high to a batter who swings up on the ball, and that a batter who chops down on the ball will have difficulties hitting a low pitch, or a ball breaking down.

A catcher must find out what kind of pitch to call for a level swinger by watching whether he pulls, steps in toward the ball, or hits standing more or less flat-footed. Naturally, I'd call for a pitch away from a pull hitter, in on a hitter who steps toward the plate, and up or down on a flat-footed hitter.

Usually I have found it best to signal for the pitcher to throw low to a power hitter and high to a weak one. There are certain batters who can hit to all fields, so when the catcher runs into this situation he has to signal to the pitcher to move the ball in or out, high or low.

If the catcher can get a hitter thinking about what the pitcher might throw, he has a very good chance of getting him out. I have found that indirectly talking to him is sometimes very effective. Now, as I've said, this is effective with some hitters, but not with all of them. Sometimes he will talk about things outside of baseball, and other times he will talk about what the pitcher is going to throw to the batter.

Personally, I like the idea of using such words as "this pitch." When a catcher says "this pitch," it puts something on his mind. He doesn't know if it will be a curve, or a fast ball, or what. This can put him in such a frame of mind that he doesn't take that real good swing at the ball, because he's started thinking and looking for a type of pitch that will not come.

A catcher must know that good hitters are going to get their share of hits, but there is always a way to pitch to each one. All hitters adapt themselves to different styles of hitting through the years and, by doing so, fall under the types I've mentioned previously. By knowing the hitter's type the catcher knows what kind of pitch to expect. Of course there are exceptions, but after playing a few games against a particular hitter, the catcher should be able to type him pretty well.

Once I played against a hitter who pulled away from the plate, yet frequently hit to the opposite field with power. The first thing I thought of was that his bat had to travel slowly. He didn't hit the ball out in front, because on the pitch he stepped in the bucket, and his bat came in contact with the ball when it was on top of him. This often made him hit to the opposite field.

A good catcher is a student of baseball, because he has to learn all about the various pitches and what makes them effective.

Why are outfielders taught to throw overhanded? Well, there are several reasons. Throwing overhanded puts a backspin on the ball, causing it to hold up in the air longer and travel more on a straight line. It is also easier to throw the ball at a lower level. This gives the cut-off man a chance to handle it more easily when necessary.

This same principle brings us back to the pitcher with a good fast ball. He is a player who puts good backspin on his fast ball. His type of fast ball travels in a straight line and in many cases moves upward, causing the batter to swing under the ball. This principle is the same as is used in the flight of an airplane. The wings are lifted up by a vacuum created on the top side. A ball thrown in the overhand manner gives a backspin that creates low pressure on the top side of the ball. Consequently, the ball moves upward. The same principle also applies to a curve ball, only it is spinning in the opposite direction. This phenomenon is known in physics as "Bernoulli's law."

Once a catcher masters these points, he can become a great receiver when it comes to working with pitchers. These things are necessary to understand and practice if an athlete wants to become an outstanding major-league catcher.

I gained this experience by catching for such greats as Satchel Paige, Hilton Smith, Barney Brown, Ted Trent, Willie Foster, Chester Brewer, and Smokey Joe Williams. I also learned a lot just listening to Bizz Mackey talk about catching. They say he wasn't the hitter Gibson was, but his overall know-how was tops. He helped me more than any other catcher I've known just by being around him for two months in the winter of '43 in Los Angeles.

One day, in a Miami hotel, some players were talking about pull hitting, and I asked Satch what he thought of it.

Satch could not sit that one out, rising to his feet to demonstrate how he would pitch to a pull hitter. He said, as he rose, "I'd rather pitch to all the pull hitters in the world than to pitch to them punch and straight-away hitters."

Pointing to an imaginary home plate, he told us, "I'd throw my fast ball out there on the outside corner with something on it, and you can bet he ain't gonna pull it. They can say what they please about pull hitters, but give me one to pitch to any day."

Satch walked over close to me and said, "Now here is a man who understands what I'm talking about, because we have played together many times."

"Well, Satch," I responded, "I think you're right, but you must look at this situation from every possible angle. How many pitchers have as much on their fast ball as you, and how many have as much control? I've never seen, or faced one yet. Some may be as fast as you, but they don't have the control you possess. And another thing. You know a good pull hitter will hit a good fast ball from the middle of the plate to the inside corner. You remember this from the home run I hit off you in Pittsburgh back in '33?"

"Yeah, but Trouppe, you ain't no pull hitter. You hit the ball to all fields. And, another thing, how many have you hit off me since then?"

Slapping Satch on the shoulder, I smiled and replied, "Well, we won't go into that." To tell you the truth I have not played more than a couple of games against Satch since '33, and in those games I don't recall getting a hit.

A catcher has to understand one thing about catching, and that is that all pitchers don't get a hitter out in the same manner. Even so, basically what I've stated still applies.

EPILOGUE

x

140

A catcher must use the same technique in thinking as a man who's playing checkers. He must know what the next pitch is going to be regardless of whether it is a ball or a strike. A catcher has the same responsibility as an army general. He has to plan his attack before each pitch.

HITTERS OF TODAY AND YESTERDAY

In the twenty-odd years I played baseball, plus the dozen or so I spent scouting, I have discussed hitters of today and yesterday, pro and con. I've talked with ex–major leaguers, and with some of the outstanding Negro stars of the period before Jackie Robinson's time. After talking to these men, I've come to the conclusion that the players of yesterday had an edge over most hitters of today. Now, I'm saying most batters, not all. I base my opinion on records and experience.

Recently we have seen and hailed such hitters as Ted Williams, Stan Musial, Hank Aaron, Willie Mays, Ernie Banks, Joe DiMaggio, Jackie Robinson, Duke Snider, Enos Slaughter, Yogi Berra, Harvey Kuen, Mickey Vernon, Rod Carew, Mickey Mantle, and Roberto Clemente.

Only seven of these players, Williams, Musial, DiMaggio, Clemente, Mantle, Carew, and Aaron, have hit above .350 for an entire season.

It is interesting to me, though a little sad, to realize that many people did not recognize the late Roberto Clemente's greatness until after his death. He was a meek-mannered young man who, in my opinion, from the first moment I saw him play, could do everything well. He was underrated during his lifetime, but following his tragic death in the crash of the mercy plane to the earthquake-stricken Managua, Nicaragua, his record was acclaimed.

Yesterday, we had players like Lou Gehrig, Babe Ruth, L. Waner, P. Waner, Al Simmons, Jimmy Foxx, Bill Dickey, Joe Cronin, George Sisler, Tris Speaker, Ty Cobb, Harry Haielman, George Kelly, Mel Ott, Bill Terry, Pie Trayner, Roger Hornsby, and many others who had higher averages than .350. I'm saying this to prove one thing. Many of these hitters had to bat against pitchers who threw a variety of pitches; curve, spit ball, fast ball, slider, change of speed, and the shine or emery ball.

Today's pitchers have only the curve, fast ball, slider, and change of pace, yet batting averages are much lower today than they were twenty-five years ago.

One of the few exceptions in modern day ball is Early Wynn, who regularly won fifteen to twenty games a season while he was playing. I caught Early in '52, and I know that he threw a curve, fast ball, knuckle, slider, sinker, and change of speed. I wonder what would happen if there were more pitchers like Early Wynn. He was still winning his twenty games at the age of forty.

There were Negro players who were great hitters like Oscar Charleston, Josh Gibson, Doby Moore, Willie Wells, John Henry Lloyd, Jimmy Lyons, Buck Leonard, Cool Papa Bell, Christobal Torrienti, George "Mule" Suttles, Raleigh

"Bizz" Mackey, Willard Brown, Jim Brown, Pete Hill, George Scales, and many others who hit against a great variety of pitching. There was one particular pitch used by many pitchers in the Negro League that really could deplete a batting average fast, and that was the shine ball—scratch, emery, take your pick. All the terms describe the same kind of pitch, and it could make even a great hitter look bad.

I played against many pitchers in the Negro League who mastered more than four different pitches. Among these were Joe Williams, Chester Brewer, Ray Brown, Ted Radcliffe, Phil Cochress, Willie Foster, Ted Trent, Leroy Matlock, and Theolic Smith.

What I'm saying is that pitchers of yesterday had more of a variety of pitches than pitchers of today, and yet the batters of yesterday still had higher batting averages.

Now, I realize that trying to evaluate the performance of players you never had an opportunity to see play is not easy. I can recall how I first felt about Torrienti, Jimmy Lyons, Bingo DeMoss, and John Donaldson, whom I never saw play. When I first saw these men in our dugout, or in the stands talking baseball, I didn't actually pay much attention to them, until later, after someone told me about them and what they did. When I talk to some of the young players of today, I recognize that what is on their minds is the same attitude I had in my early days toward players I never saw in action.

Some people like to say that the reason the batting averages have declined is because of playing under the lights, the long season, and better defensive play. However, there is more to it than that—the ball is livelier today; Astroturf will burn a player up if he falls on it, so he has to play more cautiously on it than on grass. It's true the gloves are much larger today than they used to be, but players in the old days had the skills to still come up with the big play. And when is the last time you heard of a major-league ball player going through the season averaging less than twenty strikeouts a season? In the old days if you struck out over twenty times a year you were disgraced. In 1925, as a matter of fact, Joseph Sewell established a major-league record that still stands by striking out only four times that year! Players are swinging down on the end of the bat, rather than choking the bat so they can have more control with their swing. It's a simple baseball fact. Hitters who hold their bats down on the end of the handle strike out more. Players have lost the art of choking the bat, staying alive at the plate until they get a pitch they can hit, or a base-on-balls. This is the most significant reason why major-league batting averages are declining.

SCOUTING

Drawing from my experience in pro baseball as a player, player-manager, and scout, I can state that an organization is usually as strong as its scouting staff.

Many things have proven to me that a good scout is mandatory if an organization is to develop into a top-notch team. Such a team cannot develop unless scouts associated with the organization have the gifted sense of recognizing genuine talent when they see it. It is a known fact in baseball circles that everyone looks for natural ability in a player—good arm, swiftness of foot, agility, and good reflexes. But, in many cases, these things in themselves do not spell out a true test for measuring the ability of a young player. A scout has to look for much more, and he has to know what he's looking at when he sees it.

In my first year in American Legion baseball, we had an outfielder who could do it all. But even as young as I was then, I could see the boy did not have that certain mental tenacity that every player must have if he is to improve his game as he goes along. That boy never played any higher than sandlot baseball, as I figured.

A scout is concerned about this type of boy, the kind who plays well but whose mental development does not keep pace with his physical growth. Such a boy will never play a high standard of baseball. But, because he has a natural physical ability for the game, someone is sure to sign him.

Another type of boy every scout meets is the one who does not have too much natural ability but is very alert. A boy's ability to think quickly can carry him to the top. The best example of this kind of athlete, that I know of, would be the late Jackie Robinson.

The third type a scout finds is a boy who will develop slowly but has a wonderful disposition and truly loves the game. Usually boys who will grow big are somewhat awkward at the age of seventeen or eighteen. I take myself for an example, and I've seen it in many other cases.

When I was in high school, I was very slow, and I was concerned about it. I asked my coach why I couldn't run better than I did. I was then about fifteen. He said I was just young and in that awkward stage of life. He predicted that when I was a few years older, I'd develop more and then my speed would pick up.

The fourth type of boy has everything and can hardly miss. When I was twenty-five years old there were few players in the league faster than I.

That certain God-gifted knack a good scout has to have includes the ability to understand different personalities. He must be able to recognize the four types of young players I have described. Of course, the best scout will miss on a boy sometimes, but if the scout has the qualifications to do the job, he will come up with a good percentage of major leaguers.

People have asked me what I look for in a boy. Some will ask if I look for a good hitter. Naturally, I look for a boy who shows real ability with a bat. The way I see it, good hitters are born and not made. Of course, they learn different things that enable them to become better hitters.

A boy is either born with a good throwing arm or he isn't.

Two youngsters can live next door to each other and come up through the years playing baseball together, and one will just naturally have a better arm than the other.

A good hitter has to have good vision, that split-second timing in his reflexes, and the thinking ability to know when, where, and how to swing on a pitched ball. When I say when, where, and how, I mean just that. The boy who has the ability to follow the ball all the way from the pitcher and can decide at the last split second when, where, and how to meet the ball is a good hitter.

Here is an example: A good hitter knows that a pitcher with a good fast ball, curve, slider, and sinker delivers every pitch with the same motion. Now, when the hitter faces such a pitcher, he will overhand the high pitch, swing up on low pitches, pull belt-high inside strikes, and push outside pitches to the opposite field by moving toward the plate, all in the last split second and all by instinct.

There are players who become better hitters after they play a few years in pro ball, but a good hitter is usually good from the start.

I have seen these concepts utilized by others as a young boy, and later I was able to apply them myself. The Negro League did not have scouts, and teams had to find out as much as they could as quickly as possible about a boy. They would carry extra players only a few weeks after spring training. The manager only had a short time in which to decide on a boy.

The only other way boys got a chance to make the team was by trying out during the playing season. They would come to the park and work out before the game. Conditions such as these forced Negro baseball managers to become excellent judges of baseball talent.

The time to spark the interest of a boy in baseball, in my opinion, is when he is just entering his teens. This gives him about five years to learn the game, find his particular ability in it, and develop himself. Baseball requires young men, and by the time a fellow is seventeen or eighteen, he ought to know if he wants a career in it and whether or not he has the ability.

It is my observation that while the little leagues are generally good and offer kids a lot of fun and exercise, too much exposure to baseball at such early ages can and often does destroy a boy's potential in the game because he has simply started too young and become bored with it before he has reached his twelfth birthday. Baseball requires not only young men, but also enthused and dedicated ones. I believe if a bat is first put seriously into the hands of a boy at the age of twelve or thirteen, he stands a chance of becoming a professional player, if he has the desire to do so. Start a youngster any younger and you run the risk of his losing all interest in playing beyond the days of the little leagues.

Scouting players can really begin through supervising teenage boys, a job well worth any man's time. Scouting of players for the majors is really a science, and a good scout is truly God-gifted.

EPILOGUE

IS IT THE SKIN OR THE EYES?

Playing baseball in Bismarck, North Dakota, from 1933 to 1936, was my first experience playing on an integrated team.

Something occurred there that puzzled me for years. One day just before practice, I saw one of the white players take a cup of water, pour it on the ground, make some mud, mix it into a thin, paste-like texture, and rub it under each eye, just over the cheek bone.

"What are you doing, Massman?" I asked. "You joining some Indian outfit?"

"Oh, come on, Quincy," Massman said. "You know what it's for. It cuts down the glare of the sun. The sun reflects from my skin into my eyes. With this mud, I can see better."

"Well," I laughed, "I don't have to worry about that. I've got a natural tint."

A few years after leaving North Dakota, I went to Mexico and later started playing winter baseball in the Latin countries. All during those years I remembered Harold Massman in Bismarck and the mud. While I was playing in Latin America, the light-skinned native players never used anything on their faces, and they seemed to see very well. I know that the sun is more glaring in the Latin American countries than in North Dakota, but no one seemed to be bothered by skin glare.

For years I studied this thing, but I couldn't make heads or tails out of it. Then, one day, I was looking through some record books and an interesting thought came to my mind.

It seemed that most Latin players had brown eyes. There were a few with gray or blue eyes, but the ones who had the most outstanding batting records had brown eyes.

I looked up the record of the Cuban League, which ranks next to the United States as far as organized leagues are concerned. The Cubans have records of their leagues going as far back as 1878. Their records of champion batters go back to 1885. The record I have is from 1885 to 1949.

There were only two players, according to those records, who may not have had dark eyes. In 1919 Manuel Villa of Cuba was the champion batter, and I'm not sure of the color of his eyes. But in the 1946-47 season, Lou Klein, a blue-eyed American player, won the batting crown. It appears that the natives of Cuba with dark eyes are the batting champions.

The United States records also reveal that there are more outstanding players in the major leagues with dark eyes.

I discussed this subject with a doctor, and he told me that a person with dark eyes is more likely to contact a disease of the eyes than a person with light eyes; however, it was true that a dark-eyed person could see better in the glare of the sun than a light-eyed person.

I don't pretend to know more than the baseball league records show, but I wonder—is it the color of the skin that makes the difference, or is it the color of the eyes?

SUMMARY

I'd like to make a final statement about how I saw the Negro League ball players of the past.

First, when Jackie Robinson signed to play in organized baseball in 1945, Negro baseball was at a very low ebb. Jackie, although playing only one season at Montreal, was ready for the Dodgers the next season.

Larry Doby went straight to the Cleveland Indians, in 1947, from the Newark Eagles.

Ernie Banks signed with the Chicago Cubs in 1953 when Negro baseball was even weaker. I know it is possible for an exceptional thing to happen, just as it did for Mel Ott, Frankie Frisch, and a few other white ball players who went straight from college to the big leagues. But, the point I'm trying to bring out is the caliber of baseball players we had just before my time and what happened from then up to the time of the signing of Negro players into organized baseball.

I played most of my baseball in the Negro League, and I'd say the league was on a decline at the time I started in 1931. When I speak of a decline I mean that the quality and system of play was going down in the league. Of course, there were many outstanding players developed in Negro baseball from the time I started up to the signing of Jackie Robinson with the Dodgers. There were such players as Josh Gibson, Ray Brown, Barney Brown, Buck Leonard, Ray Dandridge, Sammy Bankhead, Silvio Garcia, Hilton Smith, Willard Brown, Frank Coimbre, Perucho Cepeda, Bill Wright, Alex Crespo, Alex Radcliffe, Slim Jones, Piper Davis, Verdell Mathis, Leslie "Chin" Green, and Johnny Taylor. I don't think a single one of these men would have missed the big leagues.

During my first few years in the league, it was a great pleasure for me to listen to the older fellows talk about the players who had played before their time. I've listened to many of them, including Cool Papa, whose stories were always so fascinating.

Cool said they played the game many times stronger than it was played when I came into it. A player had to know how to duck, because the pitcher would deliberately throw at him, and there was nothing to do but drag a bunt down the first-base line. Sometimes a player would attempt to drag the ball, but the pitcher would guess his intention and the player would go down getting away from an inside pitch.

The earlier players were excellent sliders and went into bases much rougher than during my time. I recall Willie Wells telling me how he had to learn to tag in order to keep from getting spiked. He said when he first came to St. Louis to play with the St. Louis Stars, he experienced all kinds of incidents at second base. He said that after his glove was kicked between his legs and he was spiked on the hand, wrist, and arm, he decided to change his method of tagging. He would take all throws a little up the line from the base. This gave him a chance to tag the runner just as he went into his slide, or just before, which offset the danger of getting spiked.

Cool Papa was the greatest base runner I've ever seen, and I got a thrill out of seeing him get an extra base hit. He was a switch hitter who could push and drag the bunt better than anyone who played in my time. He once told me that yes, he could bunt, but that I ought to have seen guys like Jimmy Lyons, Joe Hewitt, Bingo DeMoss, Jelly Gardner, Frank Warfield, Dave Malarcher, and Bobby Williams. He said they were masters and very tricky with the bat. Sometimes they made the infielder think they were going to bunt and then hit the ball by them after the infielder pulled in close. It was a common thing then for left-handed batters to play against left-handed pitchers.

These teams had to use several sets of signals. There was always a man on each team who would figure out the opposing team's signals. They always had several fast men, and all of them could hit behind the runner and bunt.

Recalling some of the players I played against brings to mind Chaney White, one of the outstanding outfielders in the east. He could hit, catch, and throw with the best of them.

Crush Holloway was also one I saw when I first broke into professional baseball. This guy could do everything too, and when he went into a base his spikes showed like cats' claws.

Rap Dixon was a ball player's ball player. He was a big man, about 190 pounds, and could move with the grace of a man 30 pounds lighter.

Ray Brown was one of the greatest pitchers during my first years in baseball. He was one of the few pitchers I had trouble hitting in my career. At least I had trouble in my first couple of years, until I learned the strike zone. He threw the sinker, knuckle ball, curve, slider, and a real good fast ball. Ray pitched for almost twenty years. He was one of the notables of the thirties. He was also a very good hitter, and he played outfield on many occasions when he was not pitching.

Terris McDuffie was also a good pitcher with great control. Maybe McDuffie didn't play as long as some of the other pitchers, but during his time he established himself as being one of the best pitchers during the '30s and '40s.

Johnny Taylor had a rather short baseball career. I don't think he played ten years, but during that time his record was outstanding. He had good records in the United States and Mexico. I'll always remember this guy, because the only time in my baseball career a pitcher had a no-hit, no-run game against my team, it was Johnny Taylor who threw it. Johnny had only three pitches, but he had such a good curve and such a quick and live fast ball that it was pretty hard to be ready for his change-of-speed pitch when he threw it.

Hilton Smith, to me, was one of the greatest right-handers of the '30s. He had only four pitches, but threw them side-armed and over-handed. His curve ball was one of the best I've ever caught. His fast ball moved like a sinker, and he threw a slider and a change-of-speed ball. The closest to Smith's pitching style of anyone I've caught for was Sal Maglie, but though Maglie's curve was good, his fast ball was not as effective as Smith's.

Hilton Smith's fast ball was live and moved away from a left-handed hitter and in on a right-handed one. He also could really hit that ball, and the only reason he didn't play some other position after his pitching days were over was because he was slow on his feet and had awkward hands. Yet Hilton, in my estimation, had the most ability of any pitcher of my time.

Alex Radcliffe was an outstanding third baseman in the '30s and another who could do everything well. Although he wasn't very fast, he could run well enough for a big man. In anybody's league, Alex would have been outstanding.

Willie Wells was the greatest shortstop in my time, and some people say he is the greatest of all time. I guess most old-timers go with John Henry Lloyd, but I never saw him. However, when an old ball player who has seen both play tells me Lloyd is the better of the two, I will have to admit that Lloyd was a great man at shortstop.

Willie Wells was also the greatest glove man I've ever seen. His only weakness was his arm, but he played a shallow shortstop and seemed to sense just where a batter would hit. I've played with this guy and against him, and I'm certain he was a genius on knowing where to play a hitter. Because of this he didn't need a great arm to throw anybody out.

He never used a new glove in a game, but was always breaking in a new one, and when he had them broken in the way he liked he would cut out the padding. This would make his glove almost as flexible as a regular dress glove. The ball hardly ever made a bad hop and got by Wells. His reflexes were amazing. Sometimes I wonder how he would do with one of these self-catchers the infielders are using as gloves today.

In 1932 I played left field behind him with the Kansas City Monarchs, and I think he did not make over one error during the whole season.

I could talk on and on about the outstanding Negro players in baseball whom I saw during my playing days that had the agility, personality, and know-how that is found in players who stir up the fever in baseball fans everywhere.

Rube Foster had one of the greatest Negro teams. Every man on it was alert. They knew how to take advantage of any mistake the opposing team made simply because they knew and played the game so well.

One of the most interesting players I ever listened to and learned from was the noted Cuban Martin Dihigo. It was fascinating to hear him describe the plays of the game in his colorful, broken English style.

By the time I got my first chance to manage, I had been exposed to a wealth of good, solid baseball. I was successful as a manager because I was able to absorb and execute ideas that had been presented to me by experienced managers and players in the past. I also developed some ideas of my own.

At one time you could see a game with every kind of action possible going on—bunting to perfection, base stealing, hitting behind the runner, along with the home run. I think that since Babe Ruth's time there has been too much emphasis on home runs. The little man who never hits five or ten a season is down on the end of his bat, swinging for the fences. He doesn't realize that he would have so much more bat control if he choked it a little and tried to hit the ball where it is pitched.

To give an example of what the people want, and to show you that the front office of baseball isn't always right, let us consider Maury Wills of the Dodgers. Everyone went not only to see the Dodgers hit home runs, but also to see Maury Wills steal bases.

Baseball shouldn't put too much emphasis on one thing. In modern baseball most teams just play for a big inning, but if you don't have those big hitters to give you that big inning, I don't think it is too wise to keep playing for it.

In my opinion the people in the front offices of baseball should put themselves in the fans' position and realize most people come to the park to see more than just players hitting home runs.

Have you ever been to a game where three or four home runs were hit, and still the game was badly played and boring? Well, that's what I'm talking about. The people leave the park saying it was a rotten game. On the other hand, there could be only one or even no home runs hit in a very balanced game and people would leave the stands satisfied.

It's too bad the mentalities of the front offices in baseball are still so clogged up with attitudes and practices that should have no place in contemporary society. It is common talk in baseball circles now that the supply of black baseball players is drying up in the major leagues. Much of this condition, I am sure, can be traced to the attitudes relating to the hiring and developing of black talent. The deplorable practices I had to contend with in my early days of scouting for the Cardinals are still being carried on by major-league baseball clubs today.

Our great national game is patterned somewhat like our governmental system. We should get it working under the guidelines of the great principles of democracy, so that all men will be given an equal opportunity to make it to the top on the strength of their ability to excel in the game.

APPENDIX

THE BASEBALL CAREER OF QUINCY TROUPPE

REGULAR SEASON PARTICIPATION

1931	St. Louis Stars
1932	Detroit Wolverines, Homestead Grays, Kansas City Monarchs
1933	Chicago American Giants, Bismarck Cubs
*1934	Bismarck Cubs
*1935	Bismarck Cubs
*1936	Bismarck Cubs
1937	(Idle)
*1938	Indianapolis ABCs
*1939	Indianapolis ABCs; Monterrey, Mexico
*1940	Monterrey, Mexico
*1941	Monterrey, Mexico
*1942	Mexico City Reds
*1943	Mexico City Reds
*1944	Mexico City Reds
*1945	Cleveland Buckeyes
*1946	Cleveland Buckeyes
*1947	Cleveland Buckeyes
*1948	Chicago American Giants
*1949	Drummondville, Canada
*1950	Guadalajara, Mexico
*1951	Guadalajara, Mexico
1952	Cleveland Indians

*Years participated in all-star games

WINTER LEAGUE PARTICIPATION

*October 1941–March 1942	Guayama, Puerto Rico
October 1943–March 1944	Los Angeles, California
*October 1944–March 1945	San Juan, Puerto Rico; Cuba
*October 1945–March 1946	Caracas, Venezuela
*October 1946–March 1947	Caracas, Venezuela
October 1947–March 1948	Caguas, Puerto Rico
October 1948–March 1949	Caguas, Puerto Rico
October 1949–March 1950	Aquadilla, Puerto Rico; Cuba
*October 1950–March 1951	Cuba
October 1951–March 1952	Caracas, Venezuela
October 1952–March 1953	Caracas, Venezuela
*October 1953–March 1954	Cartagena, Colombia

*Years participated in all-star games

Number One All-Time Team

Position	Name	Nation of Origin	Winter League
First Base	Walter "Buck" Leonard	United States	Cuba, Puerto Rico, Venezuela
Second Base	George Scales	United States	Puerto Rico, Cuba
Third Base	Raymond Dandridge	United States	Venezuela, Cuba
Shortstop	John Henry "El Cuchara" Lloyd	United States	Cuba
Catcher	Joshua "Josh" Gibson	United States	Puerto Rico, Venezuela, Cuba
Catcher	Raleigh "Bizz" Mackey	United States	Cuba
Outfield	Oscar Charleston	United States	Cuba
Outfield	Charlie "Chino" Smith	United States	Cuba
Outfield	Christobal Torrienti	Cuba	Cuba
Pitcher	Joe "Bullet" Rogan	United States	Cuba
Pitcher	Jose Mendez	Cuba	Cuba
Pitcher	Joe "Cyclone" Williams	United States	Cuba
Pitcher	Andrew "Rube" Foster, Manager	United States	Cuba
Pitcher	Raymond Brown	United States	Puerto Rico, Cuba
Pitcher	Barney Brown	United States	Puerto Rico
Pitcher	Dave Brown	United States	Cuba
Pitcher	Leroy "Satchel" Paige	United States	Puerto Rico, Cuba
Pitcher	Richard "Dick" Redding	United States	Cuba
Pitcher	Willie "Bill" Foster	United States	Cuba
Pitcher	Hilton Smith	United States	Venezuela

Utility

Position	Name	Nation of Origin	Winter League
Infield, Outfield, Pitcher	Martin Dihigo	Cuba	Venezuela, Puerto Rico, Cuba
Infield	Willie "Devil" Wells	United States	Puerto Rico, Cuba
Outfield	James "Cool Papa" Bell	United States	Cuba
Infield, Outfield	Juan Estando "Tetelo" Vargas	Dominican Republic	Dominican Republic, Puerto Rico
Outfield, Catcher	Quincy Trouppe	United States	Puerto Rico, Venezuela, Cuba
Outfield	Willard Brown	United States	Puerto Rico
Outfield	Preston "Pete" Hill	United States	Cuba
Infield	Elwood "Bingo" De Moss	United States	Cuba
Infield, Outfield	Samuel "Sam" Bankhead	United States	Cuba
Infield	Sammy T. Hughes	United States	
Coach	C. I. Taylor		

NUMBER TWO ALL-TIME TEAM

POSITION	NAME	NATION OF ORIGIN	WINTER LEAGUE
First Base	George Giles	United States	Cuba
Second Base	Frank Warfield	United States	Cuba
Third Base	Oliver Marcell	United States	Cuba
Shortstop	Richard "Dick" Lundy	United States	Cuba
Catcher	Louis Santop	United States	Cuba
Catcher	Bruce Peteway	United States	Cuba
Outfield	Alejandro Oms	Cuba	Cuba
Outfield	Alejandro Crespo	Cuba	Cuba
Outfield	Santo Amaro	Cuba	Cuba
Pitcher	Bill Holland	United States	Cuba
Pitcher	Chester "Chet" Brewer	United States	Puerto Rico, Cuba
Pitcher	Jessie "Nip" Winter	United States	Cuba
Pitcher	John Donaldson	United States	
Pitcher	Jessie Hubbard	United States	Cuba
Pitcher	Stuart "Slim" Jones	United States	Cuba
Pitcher	Frank Wickware	United States	
Pitcher	Theodore "Ted" Trent	United States	Cuba
Pitcher	Basilio Russell	Cuba	Cuba
Pitcher	Ramon Bragana	Cuba	Cuba
Pitcher	Luis Padron	Cuba	Cuba
Pitcher	Luis Tiant	Cuba	Cuba

UTILITY

POSITION	NAME	NATION OF ORIGIN	WINTER LEAGUE
Infield	Pelayo Chacon	Cuba	Cuba
Outfield	Frank Coimbre	Puerto Rico	Puerto Rico
Infield, Outfield, Pitcher	Lazaro Salazar, Manager	Cuba	Venezuela, Cuba
Outfield, Infield	George "Mule" Suttle	United States	Cuba
Infield	Silvio Garcia	Cuba	Cuba, Venezuela
Outfield	Clinton Thomas	United States	Cuba
Infield	Perucho Cepeda	Puerto Rico	Dominican Republic, Puerto Rico
Infield	Walter "Doby" Moore	United States	Cuba
Infield	Judy Johnson	United States	Cuba
Infield	Judson "Jud" Wilson	United States	Cuba
Coach	Jim "Candy" Taylor		

OUTSTANDING PLAYERS OF THE EASTERN LEAGUE

NAME	YEARS PLAYED	POSITION	TEAM PARTICIPATION AND (WINTER LEAGUE)
Paul Arnold	1934-1935	Outfield	Newark Dodgers
Frank Austin	1944-1948	Infield	Philadelphia Stars (Venezuela, Panama)
Marvin Barker	1936-1948	Outfield, Infield	Black Yankees (Venezuela)
David "Dave Impo" Barnhill	1941-1949	Pitcher	New York Cubans (Puerto Rico)
Bernardo Baro	1916-1929	Pitcher, First Base, Outfield	Cuban Stars (Cuba)
Lloyd "Pepper" Bassett	1934-1950	Catcher	Birmingham Black Barons

APPENDIX

NAME	YEARS PLAYED	POSITION	TEAM PARTICIPATION AND (WINTER LEAGUE)
John Beckwith	1919-1934	Catcher, Outfield, Infield	Black Yankees
Jerry Benjamin	1932-1948	Outfield	Homestead Grays
Gene Benson	1934-1948	Outfield	Philadelphia Stars
Herberto Blanco	1941-1942	Infield	New York Cubans (Cuba)
George "Chippy" Britt	1920-1942	Catcher, Pitcher	Hilldale Giants
Thomas "Peewee" Butts	1938-1950	Infield	Baltimore Elite (Mexico)
Lorenzo Cabrera	1947-1950	Infield	New York Cubans (Cuba)
Walter "Rev" Cannady	1926-1945	Infield	Black Yankees
William "Bill" Cash	1943-1950	Catcher	Philadelphia Stars (Venezuela)
Porter Charleston	1927-1935	Pitcher	Hilldale Giants
Thaddeus Christopher	1936-1945	Outfield	Black Yankees
Robert Clarke	1922-1948	Catcher	Baltimore Elite
James "Bus" Clarkson	1937-1950	Infield	Philadelphia Stars (Puerto Rico, Mexico)
Zack Clayton	1934-1944	Infield	Black Yankees
Philip "Phil" Cochrell	1913-1946	Pitcher	Hilldale Giants
Homer "Goose" Curry	1930-1950	Outfield	Philadelphia Stars
Johnny Davis	1943-1950	Outfield	Newark Eagles (Puerto Rico)
Leon Day	1934-1950	Pitcher	Newark Eagles (Mexico, Cuba, Puerto Rico)
Herbert "Rap" Dixon	1922-1937	Outfield	Pittsburgh Crawfords, Hilldale Giants (Cuba)
Claro Duany	1944-1947	Outfield	New York Cubans (Cuba)
Howard Easterling	1936-1949	Outfield, Infield	Homestead Grays
Mack Eggleston	1917-1934	Infield	Black Yankees
Bill "Happy" Evans	1930-1934	Outfield	Homestead Grays
Tom Finley	1925-1933	Infield	Baltimore Elite
Jonas Gaines	1937-1950	Pitcher	Baltimore Elite
Willie "Lefty" Gisentaner	1921-1935	Pitcher	Cuban Stars (Cuba)
Thomas "Lefty" Glover	1934-1945	Pitcher	Baltimore Elite (Mexico)
Victor "Vic" Harris	1923-1950	Outfield	Homestead Grays (Puerto Rico)
Johnny Hayes	1934-1950	Catcher	Baltimore Elite (Puerto Rico)
O. "Crush" Holloway	1921-1934	Outfield	Hilldale Giants
William "Bill" Hoskins	1937-1946	Outfield	Baltimore Elite
Clarence "Fats" Jenkins	1920-1940	Outfield	Black Yankees
Grant "Home Run" Johnson	1895-1921	Infield	Lincoln Giants
Henry Kimbro	1937-1950	Outfield	Baltimore Elite (Cuba)
Harry Kincannon	1932-1938	Pitcher	Pittsburgh Crawfords, Hilldale Giants
Rogelio Linares	1940-1946	Infield	New York Cubans (Cuba)
Louis Louden	1942-1950	Catcher	New York Cubans (Mexico, Cuba)
Maxwell "Max" Mannin	1939-1949	Pitcher	Newark Eagles (Cuba)
Luis Marquez	1945-1948	Outfield, Infield	Homestead Grays (Puerto Rico)
Horacio Martinez	1935-1947	Infield	New York Cubans (Cuba)
Henry Miller	1940-1948	Pitcher	Philadelphia Stars (Venezuela)
Leroy Morney	1932-1944	Infield	Pittsburgh Crawfords, Hilldale Giants
Barney Morris	1932-1947	Pitcher	Philadelphia Stars
Alejendro "Alex" Oms	1921-1935	Outfield	Cuban Stars (Cuba)
Pedro Page	1947	Outfield	New York Cubans (Cuba)
Ted Page	1931-1937	Outfield	Homestead Grays

NAME	YEARS PLAYED	POSITION	TEAM PARTICIPATION AND (WINTER LEAGUE)
Roy Partlow	1934-1950	Pitcher	Homestead Grays (Mexico, Puerto Rico)
Lennie Pearson	1937-1950	Infield	Newark Eagles (Puerto Rico, Cuba)
Spottswood "Spot" Poles	1909-1923	Outfield	Hilldale Giants (Cuba)
William "Bill" Ricks	1944-1950	Pitcher	Philadelphia Stars
Bob Romby	1947-1950	Pitcher	Baltimore Elite
Silvino Ruiz	1928-1942	Pitcher	New York Cubans (Cuba)
Pat Scantleberry	1944-1950	Pitcher	New York Cubans (Panama)
Richard "Dick" Seay	1925-1947	Infield	Newark Eagles (Puerto Rico)
Theolic Smith	1936-1949	Pitcher	Pittsburgh Crawfords (Mexico)
Felton Snow	1931-1947	Infield	Baltimore Elite (Venezuela)
Clyde "Splo" Spearman	1932-1946	Outfield	Black Yankees
Henry "Splo" Spearman	1936-1946	Infield	Black Yankees
Paul "Jake" Steven	1921-1937	Infield	Hilldale Giants
Ed Stone	1931-1945	Outfield	Newark Eagles (Mexico, Puerto Rico)
Johnny Taylor	1935-1945	Pitcher	Hilldale Giants
David "Showboat"Thomas	1923-1946	Infield	New York Cubans
Edsell "Big" Walker	1937-1945	Pitcher	Homestead Grays
Jap Washington	1922-1937	Infield	Homestead Grays
Johnny Washington	1933-1950	Infield	Baltimore Elite
Murray Watkins	1944-1948	Infield	Philadelphia Stars
Roy Welmaker	1932-1945	Pitcher	Homestead Grays (Venezuela)
Chaney White	1921-1935	Outfield	Hilldale Giants
Chester Williams	1930-1943	Infield	Pittsburgh Crawfords (Mexico)
Harry Williams	1931-1947	Infield	Pittsburgh Crawfords
James "Jim" Williams	1937-1948	Outfield	Homestead Grays
Marvin Williams	1944-1949	Infield	Philadelphia Stars (Venezuela)
Roy Williams	1932-1941	Pitcher	Pittsburgh Crawfords
John Wright	1937-1948	Pitcher	Homestead Grays
Zollie Wright	1931-1940	Outfield	Black Yankees
Bill Yancey	1923-1936	Infield	Black Yankees

OUTSTANDING PLAYERS OF THE WESTERN LEAGUE

NAME	YEARS PLAYED	POSITION	TEAM PARTICIPATION AND (WINTER LEAGUE)
Newt Allen	1922-1944	Infield	Kansas City Monarchs
Todd Allen	1915-1925	Infield	Indianapolis ABCs
Herman "Jabo" Andrews	1930-1942	Outfield, Pitcher	Indianapolis ABCs
Daniel "Dan" Bankhead	1940-1947	Pitcher	Memphis Red Sox (Puerto Rico)
Fred Bankhead	1937-1948	Infield	Memphis Red Sox
Tubby Barnes	1922-1931	Catcher	St. Louis Stars
Sam Bennett	1911-1925	Outfield, Catcher	St. Louis Giants
Charles Beverly	1924-1936	Pitcher	Kansas City Monarchs
Charles Blackwell	1916-1929	Outfield	St. Louis Stars (Cuba)
Robert "Bob" Boyd	1947-1950	First Base	Memphis Red Sox
John Britton	1940-1950	Infield	Birmingham Black Barons
Jim Brown	1918-1942	Infield, Catcher	Chicago American Giants
Larry Brown	1919-1949	Catcher	Memphis Red Sox (Cuba)
William "Bill" Byrd	1932-1949	Pitcher	Nashville Elite Giants (Puerto Rico)

Name	Years Played	Position	Team Participation and (Winter League)
Morten Clark	1915-1923	Infield	Indianapolis ABCs
Willie "Sugg" Cornelius	1929-1946	Pitcher	Chicago American Giants
A. D. "Dewey" Creacy	1924-1940	Infield	St. Louis Stars
Jimmie Crutchfield	1930-1945	Outfield	Indianapolis ABCs
Reuben "Rube" Currie	1919-1932	Pitcher	Kansas City Monarchs
Lloyd "Bearman" Davenport	1934-1949	Outfield	Memphis Red Sox (Cuba)
Lorenzo "Piper" Davis	1943-1950	Infield	Birmingham Black Barons (Puerto Rico)
Walter "Steel Arm" Davis	1923-1934	Outfield, Infield	Chicago American Giants
Nelson Dean	1925-1932	Pitcher	Detroit Stars
William "Dizzy" Dismukes	1913-1950	Pitcher	Philadelphia Giants (Cuba)
George Dixon	1917-1928	Catcher	Chicago American Giants
Frank Duncan	1920-1948	Catcher	Kansas City Monarchs (Cuba)
Jake Dunn	1930-1941	Outfield, Infield	Detroit Stars
Floyd "Jelly" Gardner	1919-1933	Outfield	Chicago American Giants
Carl Glass	19??-1936	Pitcher	Memphis Red Sox
Leroy Grant	1911-1925	Infield	Chicago American Giants (Cuba)
Joseph "Joe" Greene	1938-1948	Catcher	Kansas City Monarchs
Robert Griffin	1934-1949	Pitcher	Nashville Elite Giants (Dominican Republic)
Lemuel "Hawk" Hawkins	1919-1927	Infield	Kansas City Monarchs
Eggie Hensley	1923-1939	Pitcher	St. Louis Stars
Joe Hewitt	1910-1931	Infield, Outfield	St. Louis Giants
Sammy T. Hughes	1930-1946	Infield	Nashville Elite Giants (Mexico)
Bertrum Hunter	1931-1942	Pitcher	St. Louis Stars
Harry Jeffries	1916-1931	Outfield, Pitcher	Indianapolis ABCs
Harry Jeffries	1920-1948	Infield	Chicago American Giants
Newton "Newt" Joseph	1922-1939	Infield	Kansas City Monarchs
Dan Kennard	1916-1925	Catcher	Indianapolis ABCs
L. D. "Goo Goo" Livingston	1928-1932	Outfield	Kansas City Monarchs
Jimmie Lyons	1911-1942	Outfield	Chicago American Giants
George McAllister	1924-1934	First Base	Birmingham Black Barons
Terris McDuffie	1930-1945	Pitcher	Birmingham Black Barons (Cuba)
Henry McHenry	1930-1950	Pitcher	Kansas City Monarchs (Cuba)
Hurley McNair	1912-1942	Outfield	Kansas City Monarchs
Dave Malarcher	1916-1934	Infield	Chicago American Giants
William "Jack" Marshall	1926-1944	Infield	Chicago American Giants
Verdell Mathis	1940-1949	Pitcher	Memphis Red Sox (Venezuela)
Leroy Matlock	1929-1942	Pitcher	St. Louis Stars
Henry Milton	1934-1941	Outfield	Kansas City Monarchs
George Mitchell	1925-1949	Pitcher	Chicago American Giants
C. "Dink" Mothel	1920-1934	Infield, Outfield	Kansas City Monarchs
James "Jimmy" Newberry	1943-1950	Pitcher	Birmingham Black Barons
John "Buck" O'Neil	1938-1950	Infield	Kansas City Monarchs
Thomas "Big Train Tom" Parker	1929-1946	Pitcher	Indianapolis ABCs
Roy "Red" Parnell	1926-1950	Outfield	Birmingham Black Barons
Pat Patterson	1934-1949	Infield	Kansas City Monarchs
William Perkins	1928-1945	Catcher	Birmingham Black Barons

NAME	YEARS PLAYED	POSITION	TEAM PARTICIPATION AND (WINTER LEAGUE)
Andrew Porter	1932-1950	Pitcher	Nashville Elite Giants
Willie Powell	1927-1935	Pitcher	Chicago American Giants (Cuba)
Alex Radcliffe	1927-1946	Infield	Chicago American Giants
Ted "Double Duty" Radcliffe	1928-1950	Pitcher	Detroit Stars
Wilson Redus	1924-1940	Outfield	St. Louis Stars
Othello Renfroe	1945-1950	Catcher	Kansas City Monarchs
Jack Ridley	1929-1934	Outfield	Nashville Elite Giants
Edward "Ed" Rile	1920-1933	Pitcher, Infield	Detroit Stars
Bobby Robinson	1929-1940	Infield	Detroit Stars
Neil Robinson	1936-1950	Infield, Outfield	Memphis Red Sox
Branch Russell	1922-1932	Outfield	St. Louis Stars
John Henry Russell	1924-1933	Infield	St. Louis Stars
Thomas "Tommy" Sampson	1940-1948	Infield	Birmingham Black Barons
George Shively	1915-1924	Outfield	Indianapolis ABCs
Harry Soloman	1925-1942	Pitcher	Birmingham Black Barons
Norman "Turkey" Stearns	1921-1942	Outfield	Detroit Stars (Cuba)
Ed Steele	1941-1950	Outfield	Birmingham Black Barons
Sam Streeter	1920-1935	Pitcher	Birmingham Black Barons (Cuba)
Joe Strong	1928-1935	Pitcher	St. Louis Stars
George Sweatt	1921-1927	Infield	Kansas City Monarchs
Ben Taylor	1913-1940	Infield	Indianapolis ABCs
Leroy Taylor	1925-1936	Outfield	Kansas City Monarchs
Olan "Jelly" Taylor	1934-1946	First Base	Memphis Red Sox
Raymond Taylor	1931-1944	Catcher	Memphis Red Sox
Sandy Thompson	1926-1932	Outfield	Chicago American Giants
Jesse "Hoss" Walker	1929-1950	Infield	Nashville Elite Giants
Jim West	1930-1947	Infield	Nashville Elite Giants
Bobby Williams	1918-1945	Infield	Chicago American Giants
Henry Williams	1922-1929	Catcher	St. Louis Stars
J. Williams	1928-1934	Pitcher	St. Louis Stars
John Williams	1943-1948	Pitcher	St. Louis Stars
Poindexter Williams	1921-1933	Catcher	Birmingham Black Barons
Jim Willis	1928-1939	Pitcher	Birmingham Black Barons
Artie Wilson	1944-1948	Infield	Birmingham Black Barons (Puerto Rico)
Burnis "Bill" Wright	1932-1945	Outfield	Nashville Elite Giants (Mexico, Puerto Rico)
T. J. "Tom" Young	1926-1937	Catcher	Kansas City Monarchs

SOME, BUT NOT ALL, OF THE SEPIA PLAYERS WHO COULD HAVE PLAYED MAJOR-LEAGUE BALL

NAME	POSITION	TEAM
Santo Amaro	Outfield	Cuba
Sammy Bankhead	Outfield, Shortstop	Homestead Grays
Bernardo Baro	Outfield	Cuba
John Beckwith		Chicago American Giants
Augustin Bejerano	Outfield	Cuba
James "Cool Papa" Bell	Outfield	St. Louis Stars, Pittsburgh Crawfords
William Bell	Pitcher	Kansas City Monarchs
Sam Bennett	Catcher	Lincoln Giants, St. Louis Giants
Charlie Blackwell	Outfield	St. Louis Giants
Ramon Bragana	Pitcher	Cuba
Chester Brewer	Pitcher	Kansas City Monarchs
Barney Brown	Pitcher	Philadelphia Stars
Larry Brown	Catcher	Memphis Red Sox
Raymond Brown	Pitcher	Indianapolis ABCs, Homestead Grays
Julian Castillo		Cuba
Perucho Cepeda	First Base	Puerto Rico
Oscar Charleston	Center Field	Indianapolis ABCs, Pittsburgh Crawfords, Homestead Grays
Phil Cochrell	Pitcher	Hilldale Giants
Frank Coimbre	Outfield	Puerto Rico
Rube Currie	Pitcher	Kansas City Monarchs
Steel Arm Davis	First Base, Outfield	Chicago American Giants
Martin Dihigo	Pitcher, Outfield	Cuban Stars, Bacharach Giants
Rap Dixon	Outfield	Philadelphia Stars
John Donaldson	Pitcher, Outfield	Kansas City Monarchs
Bill Drake	Pitcher	St. Louis Giants
Valentin Dreke	Outfield	Cuba
Frank Duncan	Catcher	Kansas City Monarchs
Bill Foster	Pitcher	Chicago American Giants
Rube Foster	Pitcher	Chicago American Giants
Regino Garcia		Cuba
Silvio Garcia	Second Base	New York
Jelly Gardner	Outfield	Chicago American Giants
Joshua Gibson	Catcher	Homestead Grays, Pittsburgh Crawfords
George Giles	First Base	Kansas City Monarchs
Pete Hill	Outfield	Chicago American Giants
Bill Holland	Pitcher	Detroit, New York
Crush Hollaway	Outfield	Hilldale Giants
Jess Hubbard	Pitcher	New York
Sammy T. Hughes	Second Base	Baltimore Elite
Jud Johnson	Third Base	Philadelphia, Hilldale Giants
Script Lee	Pitcher	Hilldale Giants
John Henry Lloyd	Shortstop	Chicago American Giants
Dick Lundy	Shortstop	Bacharach Giants
Jimmy Lyons	Outfield	Chicago American Giants
Bizz Mackey	Catcher	Indianapolis ABCs

20 YEARS TOO SOON

NAME	POSITION	TEAM
Oliver Marcell	Third Base	New York
Leroy Matlock	Pitcher	St. Louis Stars, Pittsburgh Crawfords
Jose Mendez	Pitcher	New York Cubans, Kansas City Monarchs
Doby Moore	Shortstop	Kansas City Monarchs
Alejandro Oms	Outfield	Cuba
Ted Paige	Outfield	Homestead Grays, New York
Luis Pardon	Pitcher	Cuba
William Perkins	Catcher	Birmingham Black Barons, Pittsburgh Crawfords
Bruce Petway	Catcher	Chicago American Giants
Alex Radcliffe	Third Base	Chicago American Giants
Dick Redden	Pitcher	Lincoln Giants
Bullet Rogans	Pitcher, Outfield	Kansas City Monarchs
Julio Rojo	Catcher	Cuban Stars, New York
Red Ryan	Pitcher	Hilldale Giants
Lazaro Salazar	Pitcher, First Base	Cuba
Louis Santop	Catcher	Hilldale Giants
Theolic Smith	Pitcher	Pittsburgh Crawfords
Norman "Turkey" Stearns	Outfield	Detroit Stars, Chicago American Giants
Lonnie Summers	Catcher, Outfield	Baltimore Elite
George "Mule" Suttles		Birmingham Black Barons, St. Louis Stars
Johnny Taylor	Pitcher	Pittsburgh Crawfords
Clinton Thomas	Outfield	New York
Christobal Torrienti	Outfield	New York Cubans, Chicago American Giants
Ted Trent	Pitcher	St. Louis Stars
Estando "Tetelo" Vargas	Outfield	New York Cubans, Dominican Republic
Willie Wells	Shortstop	St. Louis Stars, Chicago American Giants
Chaney White	Outfield	Hilldale Giants
Frank Wickware	Pitcher	Lincoln Giants, Chicago American Giants
Smoky Joe Williams	Pitcher	Lincoln Giants
Jud Wilson	First Base	Baltimore Black Sox, Homestead Grays
Nip Winters	Pitcher	Hilldale Giants
Bill Wright	Outfield	Baltimore Elite

1945 EAST-WEST GAME

WEST LINEUP		EAST LINEUP	
First Base	Archie Ware	First Base	Buck Leonard
Second Base	Jesse Wilson	Second Base	Frank Austin
Third Base	Alex Radcliffe	Third Base	Murray Watkins
Shortstop	Jackie Robinson	Shortstop	Willie Wells
Left Field	Lester Locket	Left Field	Gene Benson
Center Field	Neil Robinson	Center Field	Jerry Benjamin
Right Field	Lloyd Davenport	Right Field	Rogelio Linares
Catcher	Quincy Trouppe	Catcher	Roy Campanella
Utility	Avelino Canizares	Pitcher	Bill Byrd
Pitcher	Verdell Mathis	Pitcher	Roy Welmaker
Pitcher	Sam Jessup	Pitcher	Bill Ricks
Pitcher	Gene Brimmer		
Pitcher	Booker McDaniels		